Spiritual teachings received from White Cloud, a spirit guide from the White Brotherhood— helping mankind to solve everyday problems.

WALKING BACK TO HAPPINESS

by Anthea Mitchell

WALKING BACK TO HAPPINESS

Anthea Mitchell

*Spiritual teachings to encourage personal growth
Keys to unlock the doors to freedom*

2000

Copyright © Anthea Mitchell 2000

Published by
Suni Press
24 Bove Town, Glastonbury, Somerset, England, BA6 8JE

Cover photograph, "The crimson sky", by Peter O'Byrne
Logo designed by Ali, (01749) 34 62 43, email *alibaba.669@aol.com*

Designed and set in 11-point Monotype Bembo
on Acorn workstations by
Abbey Press Glastonbury

Printed and bound in Great Britain

All rights reserved. No part of this publication may be reproduced or transmitted, in any form or by any means, without written permission from the publisher.

A catalogue record for this book is available from the British Library

ISBN 0-9536180-0-5

Acknowledgments

I would like to express my heartfelt thanks and gratitude to Peter who has so patiently channelled White Cloud, and for his love and support over the years, and to Alex, who has given me her love and understanding throughout our friendship and supported me during the many painstaking hours of writing. I should also like to give my special thanks to White Cloud, who has completely changed my life by sharing his teachings.

I would also like show my love and appreciation to my two dear sons, Ivan and David, for their wonderful source of encouragement, to Colin for his important role in my life, and to all my family, especially Mum. May I mention, too, my close friends who have been there for me in my hours of need! And thank you, Tony, for proof-reading!

God Bless you all.

Walking Back to Happiness

Contents

	Prologue	9
1	The path to guilt	11
2	The miracle	19
3	Listening to the small voice within	24
4	Proof of life after death	28
5	The hermit	32
6	The hand of destiny	35
7	The perfect recipe for happiness	41
8	Every form of love is precious	45
9	The power of positive thinking	51
10	A picture paints a thousand words	57
11	The good Samaritans	62
12	Become a twinkling star in the night	66
13	Don't take it personally	71
14	The brick!	76
15	The final farewell	80
16	The storm	85
17	Separation	91
18	The four seasons	97
19	When it's right, it feels right!	103
20	An inspiration to many	107
21	Everything presented in the right order	112
22	The parting of the ways	120

Walking Back to Happiness

Prologue

To the best of my ability, I try to view life spiritually by endeavouring to see the benefits in a seemingly negative situation. By looking for the lesson it presents, it changes the experience from negative to positive. I had a tendency to judge situations at their face value. Although human, this trait served only to created unhappiness and bewilderment. Now I attempt to look deeper to see what can be learned and gained. Also, I used to go out of my way to avoid unpleasant events but now I try to face up to them with courage.

I have come to know a beautiful spirit guide called White Cloud, through the mediumship of my ex-husband and loyal friend, Peter. Over many years, White Cloud has channelled through Peter, giving many explanations as to why it is necessary to go through certain ordeals. With compassion, he has endeavoured to bring about understanding.

Having attended an absent-healing circle every week for fourteen years, I was privileged to listen to White Cloud's teachings. Over this period, he covered almost every subject imaginable and I would like to pass these on to anyone wishing to make sense of their lives.

I should like to thank my wonderful friends for their support and love over the years. Our difficulties have given us a beautiful bond and I know I speak for all of us when I say, we will always be grateful to White Cloud for enabling us see these difficulties as golden opportunities for progression. They were the stepping stones necessary for our personal growth. With this knowledge, not only were we able to help one another but he encouraged us to find our own strengths and to love ourselves in spite of our weaknesses.

Although my friends and I are there for each other, we also realise the importance of listening to our inner guidance rather than becoming dependent upon the support and opinion of others. In addition, we have come to appreciate the value of allowing time for ourselves.

White Cloud has given us practical advice with regard to coping with fears and has suggested ways of dealing with the insecurities that can cause havoc in our lives. When I learned to handle my fears, not only was I happier and more confident, but my level of self-worth increased. Also, I stopped manipulating and used my inner strength to control my emotions. This was a giant step forward.

White Cloud's teachings have helped restore my peace and harmony. This is a true account of my life and I have used it as a framework to pass on the teachings. David, my younger son, once said, "Mum, you teach by telling stories." On this occasion, I have used my own story to relay White Cloud's messages because when something is true and comes from the heart, it makes it easier for people to identify their own problems. Although my story may be different from yours, beneath the surface, we are all facing the same challenges. Therefore, I wish you luck in your life and hope that my story will serve to uplift you and give you the encouragement to persevere.

Anthea Mitchell

Chapter 1
THE PATH TO GUILT

For as long as we have air to breathe, there will be challenges! We can choose to be the victim in a tragic play or we can take life into our own hands and become the hero or heroine in a play of our own.

My whole life has been an act, pretending to be strong and confident whereas, underneath, I was nervous and unsure. This story is about finding the courage to be myself and facing up to life's difficulties rather than persuading others to change.

Although, like the majority of us, my childhood was filled with painful moments, I can now understand that the stage was being set for what was needed for me to gain an inner strength whilst still remaining soft and gentle. In other words, my formative years became the foundation on which to build my spiritual development. My parents gave me the necessary ingredients to encourage me to strive harder. If those earlier years had been easier, I would probably have relaxed and achieved very little.

The insecurities and weaknesses that emerged became my fuel for growth. My frailties were a bonus that helped increase my sensitivity to the needs of others whilst enabling me to become a stronger person. However, although it took me a long time to get to grips with this and even longer to get to know and like who I am, I don't regret one minute.

I have achieved a wonderful sense of fulfilment which has enriched my life in a way I could not possibly have imagined and, along the way, miraculous things have happened. I'd like to share these with you in an endeavour to impart the understanding gained.

At last, I regard myself as a joyful person with a deep compassion and an honest love for the people who come into my life but now I consider my own needs as well as theirs. Initially, I would have been concentrating purely on helping others because it made me feel good but it was usually at the expense of myself. Sometimes, I would be tired and wouldn't listen to the inner voice when it said, "You've done enough, now rest! Go home and put your feet up!" I'd always push myself that little bit too much. My need for love was so great that I'd never know when to say, "I've had enough."

I can truthfully say that, in this lifetime, I have achieved immense self-worth and experienced a feeling of wholeness. However, I cannot maintain it as life is continuous and, as such, new challenges are presented daily but I understand that pain is necessary for it keeps me in touch with those I am trying to help. I also know that it is important to speak from the heart and from "having been there" rather than from empty words. We have to truly "know" what another person is going through in order to respond with heartfelt compassion.

Now I say to myself, "What am I learning from this?" and, "How many other people have benefitted?" This way of thinking has brought about a tremendous transformation within me. It takes time to see the benefits but, eventually, love fills the space that was once filled with pain and peace takes the place of suffering. As uncomfortable as it may be, pain is instrumental in our quest for truth.

My story begins with my mother who was, and still is, a

brilliant pianist, having achieved the highest honours for her degree in music. Unfortunately, grandmother, having a Victorian attitude, wouldn't hear of her daughter taking up a musical career but insisted she married the good-looking man who came to the church. My father was delighted that the attractive church organist had chosen him and, as in all fairy tales, he thought that they would live happily ever after!

After the wedding, Dad was in for a shock when he discovered Mum's secret ambition to become a dance band leader. She wasn't content with playing in the church but had ideas of her own! However, she was trapped, complaining bitterly that she should never have married Dad but what could she do! Divorce was unheard of in those days and a social disgrace. Meeting James, who played the saxophone, was the best thing that happened to her. Together, they started a band and shared their love of music but, give Mum her due, she stuck by us and although she was a square peg in a round hole, she did her best.

As hard as I tried, I couldn't compete with the song in the background that seemed to be playing when I wanted us to talk. Mum was clever at listening to music and transcribing what she heard onto a music pad but then she'd become engrossed in a world of her own, sitting at the piano to perfect the tune she had captured on paper.

I wanted so much to "feel" loved by Mum. I knew she did love me but, with her preoccupation in music, I couldn't get her attention. With the constant interruption of the radio, I was unable to talk to her and ended up apologising before I spoke. However, because she appreciated my efforts to make her happy, I worked hard for recognition. "There's a good girl," or "Well done," became like music to my ears as they meant, "I love you" but, unfortunately, I became a "people pleaser" in order to gain the love and attention for which I craved. How could I possibly know at such a young age, that I could earn my own love by doing the things that made me happy instead of constantly searching for love by pleasing someone else.

Although I felt James to be the intruder in our family, I guiltily found myself liking him. He had a wonderful sense of humour and the ability to make Mum laugh, something which Dad couldn't do. However, I admired the way Dad related to people. He was a lovely man and being the proprietor of the local grocer's shop, his qualities showed in the way he cared for his customers to whom he was kindness itself. The shop was Dad's world and he loved it. And, with the gift of making everyone feel special, it became obvious that people regarded him with great affection.

Although Dad was busy, my golden moments were when we were together. At every opportunity, I'd pour my heart out to him. On looking into his soft brown eyes and seeing the concern in his face, I'd be filled with love. Someone cared and was listening to me.

Mum and Dad often rowed about their different priorities. At these times, Dad and I became really close but, although I could never admit it, when they kissed and made up I was filled with agony. They had become friends and I wasn't needed any more. Therefore, although I liked it when the family were at peace, it created conflict within me and I'd feel ashamed of my thoughts. It didn't dawn on me then, that when I was needed, I felt loved!

Also, I was dealing with other contradictions. I was proud that Dad confided in me about Mum but I was faced with divided loyalties and, although I loved Dad, I didn't always respect him because he wouldn't speak up for himself. In addition, guarding his secrets meant that I had to be secretive, which made me feel guilty. Inner peace was a luxury!

I can't remember living with Tom, my brother. It was well known he had been a troublesome child and it had affected him badly when a serious illness, which threatened to take my life, made me the centre of attention. Feeling left out and in the way, he became sullen and un-cooperative, which caused havoc for Mum and Dad. It was a sad day for all of us when his behaviour became too much for them to handle because, finally, he was sent away to a school for "naughty" boys. Feeling guilty at being the one left at home, I cried miserably and, unfortunately, it pushed an enormous wedge between us.

Apparently it was at this time that I developed an noticeable stammer. My first recollection of this was when Mum took me to a speech therapist. Whilst being asked to read aloud to assess its severity, not only was it identified to the therapist but also to me. The frightening ordeal of being unable to express myself, and the helplessness experienced, cast a giant shadow over my timid world.

Although I became an expert at avoiding the words that tripped me up, I could not avoid the suffering that resulted when I became cornered into answering direct questions. Feeling trapped, I would be consumed with embarrassment as I ploughed my way through the words that presented obstacles. School was my biggest challenge. Fearing to be thought of as stupid, I tried desperately to hide my flaw. I was sure my classmates wouldn't like me if they discovered I stuttered so I'd go to great lengths to earn their approval. Also, associating popularity with clever conversation, I was eternally grateful to anyone who became my friend knowing that I stuttered.

The fact that I could tell Dad my problems was a comfort but I didn't want to add to his worries or encroach on his time. I later realised that, if I had trusted my instincts to share when the painful experiences had taken place, I wouldn't have carried them into my adult life but, there and then, it seemed more loving to spare Dad's feelings. At the time, I was resolute that I'd confide in him when the timing was perfect and when an opportunity presented itself but, unfortunately, that day never came. On reflection, I am sure that the stammer was caused by repressing the pain, the inner conflicts experienced and feeling unable to be honest about my feelings.

My greatest source of happiness came whilst riding my bike in the country. Meandering around the lanes it struck me as odd that I found it easy to talk to the flowers and trees but as soon as I was confronted with people, my speech would block. I later learned that when we love, in whatever form it takes, we go straight to our heart centre where no fear is present. It was because I "loved" nature that I could respond to it without fear and I now realise that it was fear that created the speech difficulties. I could not have known that security comes from a heart that is filled with love, whereas insecurity comes from a mind that is filled with fear. And so many fears had entered my life caused by guilt. I felt guilty at resenting Mum's love of music, guilty for liking James, guilty that Tom had been sent away, guilty at being unhappy when Mum and Dad made up after a row and guilty about the secrets I had to keep.

My stammer became a problem that laid heavily upon my shoulders alienating me from the rest of the world. Often, I'd try to join in but wasn't quick enough and, when I did eventually speak, I was so long-winded that people would finish my sentences. Losing my nerve, I'd ask for what I could say rather than where I wanted to go. Sometimes it was amusing. I'd end up in Eastbourne instead of Brighton and, somehow, sausages always became mincemeat!

Fortunately, there came a time when I was grateful that Mum and James had a dance band. As I loved singing, the band gave me an opportunity to develop my talent but, more importantly, at last I was involved in Mum's world. It seemed that overnight, instead of being excluded, Mum and I were able to get closer through our common interest.

People were amazed that I could blossom in front of an audience whereas normally I'd be reserved. Knowing the extent of my stammer they couldn't understand how I could sing with such confidence but singing had created another form of love. It had given me the key to my heart and, from that point of safety, love could triumph over fear making anything possible.

I have since found that, however fearful I am, as soon as I get in touch with my "inner love" my fear melts and I experience a sense of freedom. I have many ways of "tuning in" to this powerful source but nature has, undoubtedly, been the easiest route.

For me, nature is a tonic and a way to get in touch with myself and when I return from a walk feeling relaxed and refreshed, I am ready to face another day. I can go for a walk feeling depressed but by tuning into nature, through appreciating everything I see, the light filters into my darkness and I become buoyant again. It's as though the mists lift and I see things clearly, putting me in a positive frame of mind, and a new life force enters, enabling me to walk forward with courage and confidence.

On seeing the transformation in me brought about by singing, Mum and Dad became contented. Tom too, having joined the Navy, seemed much happier and when he came home with his friends, it became a source of joy. Mum would cook splendid meals and both parents would put themselves out to entertain. For the first time, I felt we were a happy family.

My working life helped too. I was fortunate to have a caring employer who insisted that I read back all dictation while he waited for me to pronounce every word but it was years later that I discovered it was his way of helping me. My colleagues and I had always thought of him as strict, not knowing that beneath his gruff exterior he concealed a heart of gold. In addition, he helped by expecting perfection from my work and, with the achievement of a job well done, I started to respect myself.

Dad's ambition was to become the Mayor. Being involved with its politics and having been appointed Councillor, he showed his gratitude by conscientiously caring for the welfare of his constituents. He loved our beautiful market town and was determined that a bypass would be built to take the flow of the heavy traffic. He believed that the vibration and fumes were contributing towards its erosion. Thanks to his persistence, the bypass was built and the town preserved and, when he was elected Mayor, we were so proud of him.

It was a terrible blow many years later when the shop caught fire. Tom, now a fireman, was witness to Dad's intense agony as he watched his beloved grocer's shop go up in smoke. Being unable to pacify him, Tom had difficulty in keeping Dad from running into the flames. Devastated, Dad became ill and his stomach ulcer erupted. He was rushed to hospital and slipped into a coma and I am sure he gave up the will to live.

On the day of his funeral, not only was the church packed but the streets were lined with people who respected and mourned him as a great friend. He was a remarkable and genuine gentle-man and I still miss him. He may have had his faults but he did his best and no one can ask for more. The only thing left for me to say now is, "Thanks, Dad. You gave me so much love. You were a wonderful father and I'll always love you."

Chapter 2
THE MIRACLE

Three years before Dad died, I was desperate to get married. I had been a bridesmaid three times and, as was usual in those days, I was terrified of being "left on the shelf". It created a stigma that if a girl wasn't married by a certain age, there was something wrong with her. It's laughable in this day and age to think that there was a time when people thought this way but it was a common thing then and often youngsters were pressured into an unsuitable marriage. In my case, I was insecure and thought marriage would give me security.

When Colin came into my life, I lit up. Here was a boy who had not only been around the world, which was thrilling and most unusual in those days, but who was tall, dark and handsome and interested in me! I couldn't believe my luck. This wonderful opportunity had come my way and, to add to my excitement, he looked like my dad! On reflection, I must admit, I had been looking for a father-substitute but it didn't dawn on me until much later that just because people look alike, it doesn't mean that they are alike. I also found out, much to my disappointment, that marriage isn't a cure for insecurity.

However, with the injection of love and optimism that had

entered my veins, my stammer vanished and I became more confident and happy. Colin, captivated by my happiness, was totally unaware of the many traumas that lay before us and how unprepared emotionally both of us were for the big leap into marriage. However, we both felt that it was meant to be. He was the boy who lived down the road who, in 21 years, I had never met—but in a crowded concert, miles away from home, we were introduced to each other by his aunt. In equally unusual circumstances our paths crossed again, this time in a hospital, so we felt it was our destiny to be together.

It was a white wedding, with all the trimmings. Although I felt I was playing a part, I enjoyed dressing up and looking beautiful. However, when it was over, we quietly slipped into a little church on our way to the honeymoon to make our personal vows to each other. Being idealistic, we wanted to make it special. We had such high hopes of our marriage being different. We were not going to get stuck in a rut or allow it to become a drudgery. We were going to keep romance alive—but it was just a dream. How different reality is when faced with household chores and the tiredness that comes from daily living. Also, I had to face the fact that going into any relationship with such high expectations was totally unrealistic.

We were very immature. We didn't know how to discuss problems or how to be tactful when we wanted something. We were self-centred and viewed the world from how it individually affected us and we were faced with new emotions that we didn't know how to handle. Instead of trying to control our emotions, we tried to control each other. It occurred to me how school ill-equips us with the necessary ingredients of life. Lessons on home management, parenthood and dealing with emotions would have been far more beneficial than the ones we learnt.

Colin was interested in the Spiritualist Church and although I had some reservations, I decided to make a concerted effort to become a part of his life in order to try to improve the relationship. Secretly, I had always thought of Spiritualists as being rather "weird" but I respected Colin for his beliefs. To my amazement, ordinary, homely couples were being introduced and there was not one crystal ball in sight! Where were the strange ladies with the big round ear-rings? The church service was similar to the ones I had been used to but with the addition of "spirit messages" from the other side — whatever that was!

I was sceptical about the messages: they could have applied to anyone. I felt like a disbeliever and therefore dreaded the clairvoyant coming to me. I would keep my eyes down when the lady on the stage was looking for her next "victim". Half the time, I suspected she was mind-reading or that there was some trickery or maybe someone had told her before the service about people in the audience. Either way, I was not going to be taken in!

One day, however, taken off guard, the medium unexpectedly caught my eye. "I'm coming to the lady over there," she started. As all eyes turned to me, I froze. How I wished I could disappear. My heartbeat increased as a wave of panic swept over me. But, not wanting to look a fool, I smiled and said, "Thank you." Continuing, she asked, "Is that your first wedding ring?" "Yes," I replied. Nothing was going to stop her now. With determination, she proceeded to say, "Well, it won't be your last. I am seeing another ring being placed on your finger and I've got the number 11. Watch out for the time of the bluebells — that's when everything will change."

Feeling thoroughly shaken, Colin and I left the church in a hurry. With our marriage still in its early stages, we weren't ready to hear this and we needed to convince ourselves that the medium was wrong. A few weeks later, we were in for another surprise. This time, the medium looked at me and said, "Are you expecting a baby?" Nodding, I smiled, feeling rather pleased with myself. The audience looked delighted. I felt like the heroine in a play. "Well, it'll be the first of three. You'll have two boys and a girl." Although I didn't believe her, I still found myself looking thoughtfully at bluebells every year and naming the children before they were born!

All too quickly, I allowed Colin to become the dominant partner. I became subservient, reverting to my childhood role of trying to please. Although unaware, we were using different methods of manipulation to control one another in order to get our own way. It was destroying our marriage. We would become quiet and aloof, which had the effect of bringing our pain to the other's attention. We fell into the habit of cross-examining, frequently probing into each other's whereabouts, creating feelings of guilt and mistrust. We were quick to find fault, using "put-downs", instead of encouragement. And, to add to the guilt, we would revert to "poor me". Our energy was constantly being drained because instead of giving, quite unconsciously, we were taking from one another.

After the birth of our two sons, Ivan and David, I conceived yet again. To my dismay, the doctor advised me, for health reasons, to have an abortion. Feeling very distressed, I prayed in the church for guidance and wondered why, on that day, it was packed to the brim with "hopefuls" waiting for a message. But I soon discovered the answer when the medium gave his clairvoyance. He was brilliant at his work. To my amazement, he came to me first and with a strong clear voice started to talk with a sureness that I had never heard before. He was so dynamic and made such an impression on me that I found myself sitting upright to pay attention. I can remember the message almost word for word.

"You have just been praying — asking for help." I was staggered by the accuracy of his statement and the fact that my prayer had been answered so quickly. Feeling stunned, I nodded my reply. "Don't do anything. The situation will be taken care of. You will witness a miracle. Your guide is telling me that you worry about the future and wants me to say, start to live for today. Today is so precious, don't waste it. Tomorrow will never come for when it is tomorrow it will be today again. Time enough to deal with tomorrow's worries then. Don't dwell in the past—you can't change it. All the thinking in the world won't change what

The Miracle

has happened so live for today. Make each day a new beginning."

All he said had been true. Most of my days were ruined by dwelling in the past or worrying about the future. Thanking him, I felt a sense of relief. This man had come to me in my hour of need and, for the first time in the church, I was grateful for a message.

To my delight, the following day I woke up feeling wonderful. I poured myself a cup of tea and it didn't make me sick. I cooked myself a fried breakfast and I could eat it. My morning sickness had disappeared. I was exhilarated. I could cancel the operation. I was sure the miracle had happened. I rushed to tell Colin the good news. Although he was pleased for me, he was also sceptical. He reasoned that with the hospital appointment due the next day, there would be no harm in going through with it—just in case! I argued saying, "It must be true. I feel so good. And, I've stopped being sick." But the pressure was on and with common sense on his side, I gave way.

The day was so important to me, I remember it well. It was a Thursday! Although I was the last one to be taken into the operating theatre, to my surgeon's surprise, I was the first patient to regain consciousness. His smile and the directness of his gaze assured me of his complete honesty. "You shouldn't be awake yet but I'm glad you are. I wanted to tell you an amazing thing. Although the tests showed you were pregnant, there was nothing there. Nothing at all! It's almost as if you were never pregnant." I could see he was mystified. An inner happiness filled me with peace and, feeling that a giant weight had been lifted from my shoulders, I snuggled down under the blankets.

Whilst blissfully lying in bed, thinking about my miracle, a peculiar thing happened. The ceiling of the hospital ward seemed to take on the arched shape of a church and I could actually hear a choir of angels singing. I know it could have been my imagination but I saw it so vividly. And—I felt greatly blessed. Later that year, my closest friend gave birth to a beautiful baby girl on the day that mine was due!

Chapter 3
LISTENING TO THE SMALL VOICE WITHIN

In spite of life's difficulties, I always thought of myself as a lucky person and therefore it was no surprise when, on hearing about the part-time job with the Council, the position was offered to me! Although I enjoyed motherhood, my mind was aching for stimulation and this was an ideal opportunity to earn a little extra as well as doing something that made me feel a useful member of society, outside of family life. Mum, being supportive, took the kids off me for a couple of hours every day.

Dad was a regular member of our local church and, being none too happy with my involvement in the Spiritualist Church, was delighted to see me taking an active part in a different environment. At the office, I was fortunate to meet a caring lady who became my lifelong confidante and friend and I have often thought that without her I would not have emerged so well through my many traumas. Realising now the importance of sharing painful experiences, I see her friendship as a gift because she knew how to really listen.

In spite of Dad's fears, I continued to go to Colin's church as it had become a way of life. Even my grandmother, who was very loyal to her own church, came along to the services. Initially, she came because the Spiritualist Church was only five minutes walk from her home but, at the age of 90, I expect she was curious to see if she could receive a message from my grandfather. Also, she was probably hoping for some reassurance that they would meet again. The church brought her a lot of comfort in her old age and I am sure that making new friends and seeing me every week gave her a reason to live. It certainly brought us closer together and I missed her when she died.

At one of the church services I became interested when a medium gave a talk on "listening to the small voice within". Some would call it instinct but I later came to call it intuition (inner tuition) or my guidance from within. These feelings, described as promptings or hunches, help us with day-to-day living. I was fascinated. The medium asked us to try, for one whole week, to give ourselves over to this small voice, saying, "Really listen and act on its guidance and see what happens to you." It seemed like an exciting adventure and I, for one, wanted to have a go.

It was quite a challenge to stay alert but I knew that if I was going to succeed, I needed to try so that I would be ready to act on what I heard from that inner source. I had been so used to arguing against these promptings, always coming up with a good excuse as to why I should ignore them. Also, my mind was constantly preoccupied and had the habit of drifting off to wherever it wanted to go. Mind control was not one of my strongest points.

I decided to make use of my five senses. Maybe, if I looked carefully at what I was seeing, it would help my powers of concentration. I listened to the birds. I had never fully appreciated how beautiful their song was but "really" listening filled me with pleasure. I breathed in the fresh air more purposefully. Yes, that made me feel good too. I became aware of aromas and, in particular, the smell of freshly cut grass sent me to seventh heaven. It was beautiful.

And the smell of individual flowers: I couldn't believe just how different they all were. I started to touch the softness of the leaves and feel the wind on my face — things I had never done before. An exhilaration came from becoming one with nature.

From this time on, my life became enriched. Although, in my quiet moments, I still had to deal with the many negative thoughts that arose, I now had a way of coping when my mind went out of control. I would just go for a walk and, purposefully, take notice of what I was seeing, hearing and smelling. Sometimes, I could even taste the salt when walking beside the sea. Walking and tuning into nature became a magical time for me and a way to get back to the reality of the here and now. I always felt so much better afterwards, as though my mind had been healed. I became tranquil and could look at my problems in a different way.

It was years later, when I was fortunate enough to hear a Buddhist talk of "mindfulness", that I realised the importance of my discovery. The Buddhists believe that by staying totally in the present, one can be tuned into the inner teacher. They say that it needs to be worked at because it's easy to lose concentration by dwelling upon the problems that take over the mind. They emphasise the importance of staying alert in order to become aware of the spiritual guidance from within.

However, going back to my story, having found a way to live in the present, I was determined to listen to my small voice for a week. On arriving at the office the following morning, I noticed a smartly dressed gentleman sitting in the adjoining interview room. As was my usual custom, I introduced myself and asked if he was being looked after. Politely, he thanked me, saying he was fine and would be working in that room all week. For some unknown reason, I felt comfortable with him immediately, as though I was meeting an old friend. Perhaps it was the warmth of his smile or the twinkle in his eyes that drew me to him.

That week I couldn't do enough for the charming visitor. Happy to make him cups of tea, I was pleased when we had a chance to talk. There was something about him that was different. He felt like family. Unexpectedly, he smiled at me and said, "You're not Ken's daughter, are you? You look so much like him!" My heart missed a beat. "Yes!" Standing up, he extended his hand to shake mine. "I'm so pleased to meet you. Your dad is my godfather."

I was tickled pink! Dad had so often mentioned Robbie, his favourite godchild, and here was my first proof that my hunch was right. I had known this gentleman was someone special. It was much later I learned that hunches do, in fact, give one a "knowingness". After this we became really good friends and Dad was delighted that Robbie had come back into his life.

Another unusual thing happened that week. Whilst driving to work in the rain, I noticed a lady waiting by the bus stop. My inner voice said, "Go on, give her a lift." On listening, and being prepared to act on its guidance, I decided to respond. To my disappointment, the lady turned down my offer. Wondering what it was all about, I drove away. The next day my inner voice prompted me again and, for the second time, she refused. On the third day, I was feeling a little intimidated by her refusals but, as the inner voice persisted, I asked once more. I suppose that by now, the lady was probably embarrassed by the whole thing so she gave in.

I chattered away trying to excuse myself for badgering her and mentioned that I was going to see my father. "Does he have a grocer's shop?" she enquired. I smiled and nodded. "Is his name Ken?" Breaking into a laugh I said, "Yes." There was no stopping her now! "As soon as I got in the car, I thought you looked like him. Isn't it a small world? I'm your Aunty Pat!" As she rambled on, it was obvious that she was every bit as excited as me. I could not believe my ears. Ever since I had come to live in the village I had been looking for her, knowing she lived there somewhere. Dad hadn't kept in touch and didn't know her address. I was so pleased that my intuition had guided me to her. As an outsider, village life had been difficult to get into but I would be accepted more readily now, and Dad was thrilled too because this time he'd found a long-lost relative!

Chapter 4
PROOF OF LIFE AFTER DEATH

Little did I know that my world was about to change again. To my devastation, Dad died on my eldest son's third birthday and, as Dad was so dear to me, I needed to know for sure that there was an afterlife. Therefore, attending the Spiritualist Church took on a whole new meaning. I was now one of the people in the congregation hoping for a message and evidence that he was alive, somewhere.

There was a spark of hope when a medium said that Dad was thanking me for the red rose I was putting in the vase beside his photograph. This was true. On the advice of a friend, I had regularly cut a fresh rose as she had said that this would convey my love to him. However, although I was stunned by the accuracy of his statement, I began to suspect that he could have been reading my mind. I was grateful but came away disappointed. It was not enough.

In an effort to get close to Dad, I strolled thoughtfully to his grave. "Why did he have to suffer? I wonder if we'll meet again." There were so many questions on my mind and I needed answers. Brushing away the tears, I vowed that one day I would find out.

Help came from the most unexpected source. Colin's grandmother gave me a wonderful book called *Guide Book to the Land of Peace*. It was a beginner's book and perfect for me but sadly it is now out of print. However, what I gathered from the book, and eventually from White Cloud's teachings, is that we go to another plane of existence and, on arrival, are met by the people who have loved us and who have also passed over. White Cloud has assured that everyone is met. Also, it's a place without fear. How wonderful! When people pass over, they review their most recent life on earth to see where they have advanced towards love or missed an opportunity. Apparently, in the spirit world love is the only thing that counts.

Earth is a school to learn many lessons, and the purpose of this school is to progress towards love—but the only way to truly learn is by going through an experience. Quite often it involves pain and suffering to understand fully but, hopefully, compassion will be gained from "having been there" and compassion is another form of love. White Cloud also informs us that no one judges us at the end, except ourselves, for we only came to gain in love.

Time is nothing in the spirit world and, as people usually reincarnate to earth in groups, we meet again when we pass over to the spiritual dimension. My father and I will be drawn back together by love. The fact that most of us choose to come to earth with the same people time after time is the reason behind "instant recognition". We don't know why we like someone immediately or, to the contrary, dislike them. However, because we return to earth with people we have known before, although the outer shell changes, instinctively we know when to trust or when to be wary. Maybe the person who aggravates us is a reminder of where we once were and it's not pleasant to be reminded.

Have you ever wondered why you feel so comfortable with

Walking Back to Happiness

some people? They may be part of your soul group who you have known through many lifetimes or someone who helped you when you were in need. They may have been a good friend or nursed you when you were sick. They could have been family, whom you once loved and adored. This love is brought back, in this lifetime, for you to build on.

There is work in the spirit world, that of helping one another. When we return to earth, it is by our own choice, to progress further along the spiritual pathway. Maybe, the next time round, we will choose to be of a different gender. We may decide to be beautiful or rich or poor; whatever is required for our growth. We need to experience everything, for how else can we find the greater compassion, complete understanding and unconditional love.

It was beginning to make sense but I had a lot to learn. However, thankfully, over the years White Cloud has patiently answered all my questions, one by one.

My prayers for help were answered by our many friends from the church who gave generously of their time and knowledge. Books were showered upon me to read and, instead of just listening to the clairvoyance, I began to pay attention to the teachings. It was as though Dad's death was steering me towards a wonderful spiritual pathway. I also felt that the quality of my life was improving. However, in spite of the fact that I never missed a church service, I was still waiting for "my" proof.

One day, two mediums, a husband-and-wife team, offered to set my mind at peace by coming to the family home to give me some evidence. They were so confident that I readily agreed. The wife, Marjorie, explained that she could hear spirit voices talking to her and would see if my father wanted to communicate with me. I found myself trusting the sincerity of this gentle lady and waited in eager anticipation.

Pointing to the wall over the fireplace, she started. "Before your dad went to work, he had the habit of adjusting his tie in the mirror that used to be on the wall." Carefully, demonstrating his actions, she mimicked him perfectly. "Did he have an item of furniture in the corner of the room where he kept his account books and papers? It wasn't a filing cabinet and this piece of furniture shouldn't have been used for storing papers. In fact, he's telling me, it had another use." Her outstretched hand pointed in the direction of where the radiogram used to be. Dad used it to hide his books and papers, much to Mum's annoyance. I was pleased with this evidence because the room had changed, so she couldn't have guessed what was in it or how it used to look.

Tears began to roll down her face. "Was there a fire? Your dad's showing himself in a white overall. He says, how he wished he hadn't kept paraffin on the premises. He's worried he may have caused the fire, unintentionally, by throwing away a lighted cigarette." The fire had been front-page news, so this wasn't really evidence, but he had been worried about the possibility that one of his cigarettes hadn't been completely extinguished and I was surprised that she had mentioned a white overall. As he had been extremely proud of the fact that he had been Mayor, I was expecting him to show himself in mayoral robes. However, the white overall and cigarette gave authenticity to the evidence.

My mind was finally put to rest when Marjorie said, "Have you had an extension to your property? Your father is worried about the way a room has been joined onto the existing premises. At the top of the stairs is a dangerous section, where the staircase has been altered, making it possible for the children to have an accident as they come out of their bedroom. He wants you to build a gate so that they won't fall." When Dad had been alive, he had been worried about this and, as neither of them had been upstairs, they couldn't have known anything about it so, thankfully, I had received my proof. Marjorie had convinced me of life after death and I was now sure that, one day, Dad and I would meet again.

Chapter 5
THE HERMIT

It was many years later when I received a letter from a friend in Wales expressing a longing to talk to me. She had a problem with which she felt I could help. I was suddenly filled with an overwhelming desire to go to Wales—to be the knight in shining armour to assist my friend in her hour of need! Although it seemed impractical, the more I thought about it, the more I wanted to go. Mum, coming to the rescue as usual, looked after the boys, and made it easy for me to follow the promptings of my heart. I went straight away.

The journey, for some unknown reason, was extremely special. As I crossed the suspension bridge into Wales, I distinctly heard another choir of angels with deep voices, singing "Welcome Home." By now, I had forgotten the experience in the hospital when I had heard the choir of angels the first time and was totally filled with joy at this all-embracing wonderful welcome. Hearing the choir from both sides of the hills as I crossed over the bridge, I kept thinking, "I'm coming home." Bursting with excitement, it seemed as if I was being guided to my friend's house and although the journey was complex, I found it with such ease.

The Hermit

Sophie, my friend, was surprised when she opened the door to see me standing there. "What are you doing here?" she exclaimed, enthusiastically flinging her arms around me. "I've just written to you!" With mutual happiness, she invited me to stay for the weekend. Settling down, we started to exchange news. Suddenly, she shielded her eyes. "There's a bright light coming from you. I've never seen it before. Can't you see it?" Unfortunately, I couldn't — but I was feeling strangely euphoric. She persisted. "It's so big — and white. You're glowing!"

When we were over our excitement, we got down to the matter in hand. It seemed that the help needed was in connection with friends, several miles away. She wanted us to go there and talk to them, together. We decided to go straight away and on our way, I noticed how at home I felt as we drove past a nearby mountain. It was then that Sophie told me about the legend of the hermit who had lived in a cave on that particular mountain, hundreds of years ago. Apparently, he had put stepping stones in the river so that people could cross to receive healing from him. Instinctively, I knew that I was this hermit. Throughout my entire life, when upset, I had repeatedly said, "I want to be a hermit in Wales!" Later, it was, in fact, confirmed by a medium who specialises in past lives.

It seems that sometimes we are mysteriously drawn back to a place which has had a special meaning for us so that the memory of that lifetime can be reactivated in us. In my case, I was soon to become a healer again and the knowledge and experience gained in that previous incarnation would benefit me now.

On reflection, in this lifetime it has never felt right to tuck myself away in a secluded country cottage because some part of me knew that my hermit days were over. Having lived one type of existence, there's usually no need to experience it again. This time round, I have needed to be with people. We never really know why we have strong feelings to do or not to do certain things or why, in fact, we say some of the things we do. I am sure

33

they are throwbacks from a previous life. However, this incident certainly served to deepen my curiosity about things that had never crossed my mind before.

Chapter 6
THE HAND OF DESTINY

Unfortunately, Colin and I weren't experienced enough to put things right in our marriage and, although it was doomed to fail, we learned a lot from our mistakes. However, the breakup was assisted by a mysterious set of circumstances which I would like to share because it proves that behind the scenes there is a greater force at work.

When I was with Colin all those years ago, I was so depressed at the mention of divorce that I couldn't sleep. My thoughts were not only irrational but suicidal. I felt I was a failure because divorce had never happened in our family before. My parents had been through thick and thin but had stuck together. Then, my stammer had returned, alienating me from the rest of the world, and I'd be thinking, "Why can't I be like everyone else?" How I envied the TV newsreaders. They looked so confident and their words flowed. To the outside world everything was fine. But I was cracking up.

I can remember thinking, "What now?" However, from somewhere in the back of my mind Marjorie's words came back to me. Being such an excellent medium, I trusted her completely. "There will come a time when you will need help and when you do, phone me." Thoughtfully, I found myself wondering if this had this been predicted. I decided to phone her and, thankfully, her reassuring manner pulled me out of the abyss.

Marjorie suggested that we meet on the Sunday in her favourite Spiritualist Church so I immediately had something to hang on to but, in the meantime, she promised to ask her absent-healing group to send me some healing thoughts. I must admit, I had never heard of this but I was intrigued and, to my surprise, I slept soundly that night for the first time in ages.

Although it was nearly Easter, Colin and I drove for miles to the church in the snow but it didn't matter because for some unknown reason I was feeling optimistic. It had been a relief to be honest and to admit that I needed help and it was a comfort to know that someone cared. On arriving, we discreetly slipped into the back of the church ignoring Marjorie's welcoming signs to join her at the front.

Colin was not in the best of moods as, understandably, he couldn't bear the thought of our private life being discussed in public. Allowing my thoughts to drift during the service, I felt sorry for him. Due to his unhappy childhood, the one-to-one relationship for which he had craved had been denied and I was sure that my closeness with the boys had made him feel insecure. In that moment, a wave of love swept over me. He had always tried his best but was constantly tired and perhaps he would have coped better if he had known the luxury of a good night's sleep.

After the service there was no escape. Marjorie beckoned us and we were introduced to her healing group of six, explaining that they were awaiting a seventh member. Little did I know, I was to be the seventh! Finally, we were introduced to a healer called Peter. In a gentle voice, he asked me to place my hands into his and, whilst looking into eyes that revealed the compassion he felt, it seemed natural to respond. The strange thing was that, although the church was cold, beads of perspiration formed on my face and my hands became clammy. Also, unexpectedly, I came out in a hot flush. I was embarrassed but he said, "Don't worry. Your inside has been knotted up and now the tension is being released. After this, you will feel relaxed and your speech will flow." The healing took effect immediately and afterwards, I felt as though I had been tranquillised.

I remember so well our farewell to the group. Being so full of gratitude for the fact that my speech was flowing again, I kissed everybody lightly on the cheek but, on kissing Peter, something unusual happened. I lit up! It was as though a switch inside of me had been flicked from off to on and after the intense darkness of my depression it was wonderful to be glowing. I came away happy and in a state of bliss that lasted for weeks. I can only explain that I was walking on air and the world seemed fluffy and bright. Something had taken place that was beyond my comprehension.

Quite by chance, a few weeks later Peter and I met again in another friend's house, in a village many miles away from home. It was as though we were meant to meet. Colin was with me and on hearing me laugh for the first time in ages, he became fretful and insecure. The curious thing was that both men worked shift duties and the likelihood of their shifts coinciding was yet another miracle. I must admit, I was drawn to Peter straight away. Maybe it was the twinkle in his eyes but, for whatever reason, I enjoyed his company.

Shortly after this, we were invited to another evening where everybody could discuss their spiritual points of view. To my delight, Peter was there again and he had such a brilliant sense of humour that I found myself laughing, wholeheartedly. Colin and I had missed out on this side of life, becoming very serious in an effort to prove that we were grown up. It hadn't dawned on us that childlike fun and laughter are gifts to be treasured and that it isn't necessary to look mature. By the end of the evening, Colin was distressed. I had no intention of hurting him but it had frightened him to see me buoyant and, although we had talked about divorce, suddenly he felt threatened.

On our way home, Colin and I talked things through and

decided to have another go at making our marriage work. For the first time in ages, he became attentive again and I was completely happy thinking that our problems were over. In addition, it was spring, and the month of May always filled me with delight. The bluebells had a way of beckoning me and I would love to go off to the woods. However, whilst having a walk one Sunday morning, admiring the blue haze that stretched out invitingly, it suddenly occurred to me that perhaps Marjorie would like to know how we were getting on. Without a second thought, I found myself heading in the opposite direction instead of driving home. I wanted to tell her my good news.

As usual, Marjorie was attentive and, after my visit, she waved me off with words of encouragement. However, although I had enjoyed the morning and felt peaceful and relaxed, my happiness was short-lived. To my amazement, Colin greeted me with frowns of disapproval. He thought I'd been to see Peter! I couldn't believe what I was hearing when he said he'd never be sure where I was any more and that the marriage should end before he got hurt. In one swift moment, my world crashed around me.

I didn't feel good about not being trusted but, on reflection, I think that Colin was running from the insecurity he felt. Rather than growing through the pain it was easier to run. However, as I was drawn to Peter, I was keen to meet him with a view to starting a relationship so, with Colin's blessing, Peter and I met to discuss it. The boys and I needed a home and it seemed natural to talk about the possibility of our moving in with him. It was so simple and although it seemed sudden, it was the right thing to do. There was no doubt in my mind.

Once more, it was as though I was under some sort of spell because everything happened so easily and instinctively, I knew that Peter and I should be together. Therefore, as the hand of destiny was at work yet again, I wanted to make it special. Putting on my favourite dress and making a posy of bluebells, I took our Bible over to Peter so that we could bless our union.

However, before I left Colin, I lay awake at his side for the last time. I was suffering with a piercing headache and felt as though I had a crown of thorns on my head. I phoned the doctor and, to my amazement, he recognised my voice. After listening to my story, he felt that I was suffering with an emotional headache and advised me to go back to bed but before he put the phone down, he said a peculiar thing: "I'll pray for you." It struck me as rather odd.

On going back to bed, I pressed both sides of my head in an attempt to relieve the pain but the stabbing intensified. Holding it tighter I cried out, "Help me!" Suddenly, over my body, an angel appeared and as strange as it may seem, I wasn't frightened. I was just totally overwhelmed with the wonder that was before me. The wings were white and thick and, edged with a faint line, every curve distinct. The feet were immaculate and placed together, pointing down to reveal delicate toes. The expressive hands, with long and elegant fingers, were joined as if in prayer. I couldn't see the face, as the glow was too intense. I have never seen an angel before and, to this day, I never have again — but it was a truly wonderful experience.

Colin tried to see it but couldn't. He could tell from my expression that it was real to me, especially, as I was pointing out every detail. Perhaps it was meant for my eyes only. However, what fascinated him was the calming effect it had on me. I then closed my eyes and fell asleep and when I awoke, both the angel and the headache had gone!

Leaving the family home was a personal sacrifice. The house had been Mum and Dad's pride and joy but if Peter and I were to start afresh, I felt it appropriate to move to where we could make a new beginning. On closing the door I left a big chunk of my heart behind. I could take the memories but the tangible security that the house had offered needed to be cast aside.

Although I mentioned earlier that my marriage to Colin was "doomed to fail", I now see that it was a success. We have become such beautiful friends and although we had to part in order to grow, our time together was a necessary part of that growth. Colin was the one who encouraged me to explore the spiritual side of myself and although I never became a member of the Spiritualist Church, it played an important part in my life. It gave me a place to start my search for the deeper meaning of life and, thankfully, pointed me in the right direction.

Chapter 7
THE PERFECT RECIPE FOR HAPPINESS

The kids and I found ourselves in an entirely different world. Peter's flat was like a doll's house and I found myself playing tea parties and, for the first time in my life, felt in touch with my inner child (although I didn't recognise it as such!) In fact, we were all childlike. It was a magical world of wild flowers, of helping neighbours, of fun and laughter, of picking mushrooms and becoming one with nature.

Peter and I would go for a stroll around the block every evening, talking to the neighbours whilst the boys tried to get to sleep in the lounge. Then for hours, we'd sit listening to classical music, which raised us to another dimension, and the sunrises and sunsets seemed to come and go just for our benefit. We didn't go to church but simply prayed before we went to bed, which added even more to our beautiful existence. It was one of the happiest times in my life. I was in paradise and never wanted to leave.

When I looked at Peter's cuddly shape I would be reminded of a garden gnome so he became known as Petergnome, and I was called Fairy, which suited the pair of us. Although I had a practical side, I preferred to play. I was at my happiest riding a bike, wandering around the bluebell woods and taking the kids to watch the rabbits. For the boys' birthday parties, we'd round up their friends, go over the hills with our sausages and a frying pan and, after having fun gathering wood, would make a wonderful campfire. Here they could be happy and free to run wild.

In our doll's house, spontaneity was the name of the game. Coming very much from the heart, we would do whatever popped into our minds. We didn't have much money but it didn't matter. We'd walk and talk and share, and would smell the flowers and marvel at the clouds. What a perfect recipe for happiness! Everyone wanted to be with us because we were so happy.

It was months later when I remembered a medium's prediction, "One day, the name of Fairy will mean something to you." Isn't it amazing that our lives are so planned? If only we could grasp this concept perhaps we'd let go of worrying about tomorrow and just get on with today.

We were in for a big surprise when Marjorie invited us to tea. It didn't seem important to dress up so we were dumbfounded when we walked into her lounge to find that it was a surprise celebration party. She'd gone to such a lot of effort and had iced a marvellous cake, decorating it with a tiny vase containing bluebells! Instantly, I remembered the prediction of eleven years ago when a medium had said that my life would change at the time of the bluebells and had given me the number 11. I hadn't given it a thought but it was almost 11 years and, as predicted, Peter had given me a new ring!

It was a sad day for us when Peter came to the conclusion that we should move from the flat in order to give the boys a room of their own. I put up such resistance but, in my heart, I knew it was the right thing to do. The fact of the matter was I didn't want to leave our magical world but I now know that everything is planned. It seems my whole life has been a fairy story, purpose-built, to pass on the spiritual teachings with simplicity. I have a great need to be honest, so because these things really happened, I can write from the heart.

I had it in mind that I would like us to find an attractive old-fashioned bungalow which needed renovating. This way we could choose one with plenty of character. I wanted roses around the front door, heather in the grass, and trees that blossomed with pink petals, and it had to have a peaceful atmosphere to complement Peter's healing. In our favourite village, we found the perfect home in a wonderful setting only five minutes from the sea and within easy reach of the Downs. My dearly loved family home had been replaced by another and because it was just as enchanting, I had lost nothing.

I felt as though the bungalow had been waiting for us as the sale went through so easily and, to add to the wonder of how well things work when guided from the heart, I met an old friend who offered to do the conveyancing without charging. Soon after this we were made aware of how fortunate we had been to receive this friend's help because, a couple of months later, he died.

Peter and I felt we needed a family holiday but as we couldn't afford much we went to Minehead out of season and ended up having the wettest week on record! However, the unseen hand of guidance was about to go into action again. Whilst sitting in the car wondering what to do on that chilly wet evening, Peter wound down the window to discover that we were parked outside a Spiritualist Church! We were doubly amazed to see that we were in perfect time for the church service. Therefore, with nothing else better to do, it seemed a good idea to go in.

It felt strange to suddenly be sitting in that quaint church. Whilst deep in thought, marvelling at the coincidence, Peter brought me back to reality with a nudge. The medium was trying to catch my attention. "I'm coming to the lady over there," she started. "Do you remember a lady in spirit, who passed with a throat condition? I believe this lady was a nurse. She is telling me that a spiritual vacancy has been offered to you but you are too frightened to accept. She says, don't worry about anything. She looked after you when you were a child so she will look after you again. This is an opportunity for you to be in service and is part of the plan."

I found myself wondering what plan but was far too nervous to ask. Therefore, I thanked her for the message and left it at that. However, what she had said had been true. As a child I had been seriously ill and this nurse had lovingly pulled me through. Also, I knew that she had died from throat cancer. Peter's absent-healing group had asked me to become its seventh member but I had declined, because I was scared. This type of thing was new to me and I didn't feel ready for such a commitment. However, on giving it some thought, I decided that if this nurse had gone to so much trouble to save my life, the least I could do was to trust that she would look after me again.

This was the beginning of many years of service with Peter. A week after joining the group, White Cloud started to channel through him, thanking me for overcoming my fears. He also mentioned that they had been waiting for me for a long time and I was, in fact, to become the note-taker.

Chapter 8
EVERY FORM OF LOVE IS PRECIOUS

To my relief, the first absent-healing evening turned out to be extremely pleasant and although I was nervous, the members greeted me with warmth and affection. On admiring the beautiful flower arrangement in the room that had been set aside for the meetings, it was explained that a tranquil atmosphere was essential and that a lot of effort had been put into keeping it peaceful. Even the television had been allocated to another room but I had to smile: the cat was allowed in because it was friendly!

We were asked to meet every Tuesday evening at 7 o'clock, come rain or shine, so it was obvious that we were expected to be dedicated. We were requested to leave our worries on the doorstep and to speak with gentle voices. I was informed that this was not a development circle but a healing one, held for the upliftment of the world and for all sick and suffering people everywhere. In addition, we were seven in number as this was the number of spirituality but it could not be open circle, for anyone to attend, because it was important to maintain the same vibrations. This meant that I was a probationer.

The energy generated during these evenings was so intense that the guides used it to restore peace and harmony to the world and to answer prayers of distress. As the circle had been running for over ten years, I was privileged to join. White Cloud explained that it was a wonderful way to serve humanity so I was determined to do my best.

Firstly, we were asked to update the special healing book that contained the names of the people needing healing and then to sit in an appointed upright chair that had been placed with others to form a circle. It was thought that if comfortable chairs were used, we'd fall asleep! The healing book was then placed in the middle of the group.

To help us unwind from the journey and the day's events, we listened to beautiful music and, with reverence, commenced and closed with a prayer. To help us concentrate, the room was darkened and whilst sitting around the soft glow of an orange light, which represented a candle flame, we were asked to still our minds. It was difficult at first but, when I got into it, thinking of others in a loving way gave me tremendous peace.

It was wonderful when White Cloud started to channel simple "down to earth" teachings through Peter. It was fascinating because he addressed all the issues relevant in our minds, as if he knew what was going on. I now realise that, as a guide, he did!

With the assistance of White Cloud, life took on a new meaning. I was proud of my role as the note-taker, so after taping the messages I typed them out and circulated them to as many people as possible. I was thrilled that I had been given such an important task because not only did it help others but it helped me too. By putting the words onto paper, I was putting them into my mind and, through the very nature of the work, I had to understand what I was writing. If I couldn't, White Cloud would elaborate the following week. It was as though I had become his disciple. Also, when appropriate, Peter and I passed on the messages through the course of healing.

One day, loving parents brought their 15-year-old son,

Michael, for healing. He had suffered with cancer since childhood and, because his legs were so weak, used a wheelchair. He was always smiling and cheerful, in spite of the fact that he had been through years of chemotherapy. Both parents, and Michael, radiated a special light. I had never seen it before but, for the first time in my life, I recognised "pure love".

With determination, Peter and I went to work on improving Michael's quality of life. It was to everyone's amazement, including the doctors' and nurses', when his legs strengthened but it didn't happen overnight. It was a slow process but, in a couple of years, he was taking driving lessons. Unfortunately though, due to the fact that his immune system had broken down, he died from another illness. However, throughout the time he was receiving healing, his parents were helped to view life differently.

When the sad day came, Michael's parents were an inspiration. They demonstrated to the world, by holding their heads up high, that they knew they would see Michael again. Soon after his death, White Cloud gave this message of comfort:

> ☐ There are those who come across the divide to us, who we welcome with great love. We feel tremendous compassion for the ones left behind and understand their tremendous sorrow and bereavement, for where there is love and that love is divided, an enormous vacuum is left but, as you know, we travel from life to life. It is hard to understand why young children should suffer so much but there are reasons, and it is for each individual alone to know. They may have come for an allotted time to learn specific lessons or it may be that they have chosen to be in service to others, to give them a key to unlock the doors of compassion and selflessness, overriding all human frailties. Blessed are you who have this compassion, for you are allowing your love to grow beyond all human bounds.

Will you tell them, we hold him near. He is within our love. Our love is as great as theirs, for he is our child too. He has complete joy and happiness now. ☐

It was about this time that our dog, Emma, died and, as unbelievable as it may sound, I could identify with our friends' bereavement because of the love I felt for Emma. It was the first time I had ever loved an animal so completely. I was pleased that Michael had known and come to love Emma because I felt that he would be there to meet her. White Cloud gave Peter and me some words of comfort:

☐ The animal kingdom is as real as yours but you can only call an animal to you in the spiritual world through the power of love. If you have gained their love, they will be there to greet you, showing themselves to you as you once knew them. You can never lose love for it is the only thing you take with you from this world of earth.

Animals come to you in service and, although you may think you have chosen them, they have in fact chosen you. They are part of your pathway and are here to teach you discipline and to remind you that they are in your safe care and keeping. However, it is not a one-way thing because they learn your ways and get to know how to reach inside you and, in so doing, become a part of you.

Animals are as much a part of your life as your children, for you are their custodians. They have been given to you to cherish and feed and to find humanity and love. If you were to recount through the days with the animals you have loved, you would remember that they aggravated you, and made you do things above and beyond your normal wants, and how you had to return early from something that you were enjoying. You will also recall how you could not go here or there because of

Every Form of Love is Precious

their demanding love and because of the disciplines that they imposed upon you, without words, with just a look! That is why I say, they have chosen to be in service to you.

It goes without saying that they have taught you many lessons along their small pathways but, above all, they gave you an honourable love. Their love was honest. If they did not like what you were doing they did not conceal it, as you who are privileged human beings can do. An animal will not pretend and yet will always forgive and go on loving you. It is because of their love that they have the ability to get into your hearts and minds and to win you from lifetime to lifetime.

You may not have realised but animals are a communication between souls. They make links of understanding beyond human frailties so is not their love divine? Do you think that they are lesser than the children of the Father? Perhaps this is another meaning of "in my Father's house there are many mansions"—many kingdoms. ☐

In addition to feeling reassured that we would meet Emma again, I did not feel so guilty at comparing my loss with the loss of Michael. It's true, Emma may have only been a dog but the love that passed between us was so pure that it was just as meaningful in its own way. At the end of the day, love is love and the loss of any love is hard to bear. Many would disagree, especially those who have never had the opportunity of opening their hearts to this type of love.

Initially, this kind of love didn't happen to me. At a child, I had a dog but its love didn't touch me—it was just a dog. Emma was the first dog that had the ability to stroll right into my heart and until I had experienced the love and loss for myself, I would never have thought it possible to grieve in such a way. It takes a special pet to open the door of love but once it has been opened, it's difficult to see a dog as "just a dog". It becomes a bundle of love on four legs!

If you have not experienced the love of an animal I hope that, one day, you will because it is so beautiful. Yes, there will always be aggressive animals but there are aggressive people too and, perhaps, we shouldn't judge because we don't know what that animal or person has been through. All I know is that there is good in everyone and everything and with the power of love all things can change.

Chapter 9
THE POWER OF POSITIVE THINKING

Having moved from the flat to a family-sized bungalow, we felt the home seemed extremely empty so I suggested going back to work in order to buy some furniture. It's not like me to get a newspaper but, as was usual when my life was about to change, I found myself behaving out of character. The thought to buy one entered my mind and, on browsing through, I noticed a small advert that said, "Typing duties for bank." Instinctively, I knew that I was meant to apply and, although I was shy on telephones, the feeling was so strong that I phoned immediately.

It was a strange interview because the lady who vetted me broke down and cried. Apparently her father had just died. I reassured her that there was life after death and we discussed it at length. Through her distress we formed a bond and, as you can guess, I got the job.

I was happy at the bank because not only did I enjoy the work but Peter and I established most of our healing contacts there. If anyone mentioned that they, or their family, were ill, I'd send them along to Peter. We didn't charge for healing so the manager could sleep easy knowing I wasn't touting for business. We just loved people and wanted to help them and it gave us an incredible amount of pleasure healing the sick. And, in addition, the friendships formed were worth far more than money could buy.

It wasn't long before our home was buzzing with people coming to and fro, not only to receive healing but to talk about the messages. Sometimes we'd arrange an "open evening" for youngsters to put their own questions to White Cloud. After feeling his presence, many would become committed to the spiritual pathway, often taking up healing themselves or being drawn to some other type of alternative therapy. The workplace gave me an ideal opportunity to meet people.

Although I enjoyed secretarial work, I found myself longing to have customer contact and envied the cashiers who could express their sense of humour whilst serving. I knew that, if I could be behind the counter, I'd be good at communicating. Peter and I still went for our daily walks together as it became our "togetherness" time and was as essential to us as our food. So many problems were ironed out during these walks and the molehills that could have become mountains melted away. In fact, by the end of the walk, I'd often be skipping alongside Peter and, much to his amusement, I'd break into the "Gay-Gordons"! Although he'd be embarrassed, he'd loved it because it was all part of the fun.

Although our desire to help was genuine, I think it was our lighthearted approach that made us popular in the healing world. People with the most serious of illnesses would go away happy. Peter had that special magic that would light up a room and his sense of humour always won the day.

Our village had the quaintest bank I had ever seen and I longed to be a cashier there, where I could come into contact with our neighbours. I wanted to spread the healing work far and wide and, for some unknown reason, I had compassion for the elderly who may not have had someone to talk to during the day.

The Power of Positive Thinking

I thought that, if I was the local cashier, I could spend a little time with them.

I hadn't heard of the power of positive thinking and it hadn't dawned on me that most of my wishes had been granted when I'd been positive about what I wanted. Every time I had needed a job for a specific reason the right position had turned up and when Peter and I had been looking for a bungalow we had found the perfect one, without any effort! Much later, I learned that we can create almost anything with positive thought.

It was wonderful to wake up and actually enjoy going to work and, as usual, I was glad it was Monday morning. Little did I know that today I was going to witness a miracle. A telephone call from the lady who interviewed me was about to change my life. I was to be transferred to the village bank to learn cashiering and, in addition, I could work part-time. I couldn't believe what I was hearing. Apparently I had made my desires known at the interview and she had remembered. She said she had been so grateful for my help that when the vacancy turned up she'd thought of me.

The fact that I could now work part-time meant I was free to assist Peter with healing in the afternoons and, although I was sad to leave my friends, I knew that this was the opportunity of a lifetime. Within weeks I had settled into my new branch and, knowing nothing about cashiering, I decided to take home the guidelines on "training to be a cashier". Being so keen to do well, I wanted to prepare for the cashiering course and to familiarise myself with counter procedures.

One morning I arrived at work with the cashiers book tucked under my arm and, to my amazement, I was greeted with, "Do you think you could give a helping hand to another branch? They have no cashiers and are desperate." Instantly I replied, "They must be desperate if they want me!" He smiled, saying, "I know you've had no experience but with reading the manual, you'll have some idea and it's really only a matter of common sense." My natural instinct was to run and hide but I was used to putting on a brave face so I grinned and accepted the challenge.

Although I was in a strong mood, on the way to the branch I started to panic. I wasn't used to customer contact, let alone dealing with money, and I wasn't sure if I would have the confidence to say no if necessary. On arriving, I sat in the car park not knowing what to do. I wanted to run away but my pride wouldn't let me. My heart was pounding so I tried calming myself by breathing deeply. It struck me as odd that all this was going on in a car park. I was having a mental trauma and no one knew! However, as usual when placed in a tight corner, I prayed!

A few weeks prior to this, White Cloud had suggested seeing everything as an experience and looking for the gain rather than allowing fear to take over. I closed my eyes, letting my mind drift, "I'll be able to make more friends and dealing with the public will be good experience for me. It'll make me grow stronger too." Yes, I could see the advantages.

White Cloud had also mentioned about going with the flow of life by seeing it as a river and how necessary it was for everyone to swim in the middle in order to grow rather than playing it safe by clinging to the sides. He had explained that, although the challenges could create uncertainties, the adventures would be exhilarating and exciting. I could see that this was an opportunity to swim in the middle!

I'd been clinging to the sides for far too long, observing others taking their giant leap forward, but now it was my turn. What could I lose? Only my pride! I heard myself saying, "Go on, it'll be a bit of a laugh." So, once again, I put on a brave face and set off to face the day.

When I came away, I had gained a lot by "going with the flow". I also discovered that to win or lose, succeed or fail, made little difference as to how I felt. The stimulation received from "having a go" proved to be the reward in itself. I had grown and the rest didn't matter!

White Cloud's teachings helped me so many times to get

The Power of Positive Thinking

through difficult situations. I soon learned that, by changing my attitude I could change my approach to whatever was happening and consequently I became happier. Instead of fearing change, I was beginning to relax and enjoy life. New doors were opening and I was not afraid to walk through.

Monday was a busy day at the bank when customers paid in their weekly takings. However, in my new role as cashier, I was flummoxed when a lady paid in an enormous credit. Unaccustomed as I was to dealing with large sums of money, I could see that this was going to take a long time. She waited, patiently, as I ploughed my way through the untidy pile. Trying not to panic, I stacked it into neat bundles and started to count. Out of the blue, a colleague's voice penetrated my deep concentration and, as you can guess, I lost count and had to start again. At the time, I could have nearly died with embarrassment but the customer said, "We all have to start somewhere."

I was surprised, therefore, when the following week the lady didn't come in herself. On enquiring as to her whereabouts, I was informed that she had suffered a severe stroke and was in a coma. The staff were devastated. We had all liked her and as she was only in her early 40s, with a young family, it was unbelievable. Apparently she had been a "breath of spring" every Monday morning. As I was new to the branch, I didn't know how my colleagues would react but decided to tell them about the absent-healing circle. To my amazement, instead of thinking it weird, they asked if they could help.

I explained that they could help, from home, by sending out their thoughts of love and healing but first of all they would need to become relaxed, perhaps by listening to their favourite music. Then, it was important to pray, asking for the healing to take place, and then to visualise her surrounded by a gold or white light or, if they preferred, to imagine her surrounded by rays of sunshine. After this, they could then send her their own loving thoughts.

I would like to mention that, sometimes, I see a column of

55

light in which I place the person and if I have had a good absent-healing session, and have been able to let go of earthly thoughts, I feel wonderful afterwards, filled with peace and contentment.

My colleagues were eager to go home from work in order to do some absent-healing themselves. The following day, they told me that they had enjoyed the experience and, in addition, it had given them a good night's sleep! Also, it had been beneficial in helping them relax, leaving them feeling peaceful. It gave us a beautiful bond of friendship.

I loved cashiering. We were meant to have a marketing list for names of useful contacts but the staff were tickled pink when they discovered that my list contained names for the healing book. Also, it created a stir when, on becoming familiar with the customers, I called them "darling" or "sweetheart" and my "good-byes" were accompanied with "Bless you!" The manager, being worried that it could cause offence, thought I should be more formal but, thankfully, so many people remarked on the friendly service that he asked me to continue. The elderly villagers loved it and I was delighted when I became known as "the kind lady at the bank"!

Chapter 10
A PICTURE PAINTS A THOUSAND WORDS

A few years later, I was going through a "bad" patch at home. I was suffering with bouts of insecurity and, although I wasn't aware of it, my childhood traumas were beginning to catch up with me. On one occasion I felt quite panicky when, in the middle of a healing session, I heard Peter say, "Don't worry, you know we love you." Under normal circumstances this wouldn't have bothered me but for some unknown reason my alarm bells were ringing and I couldn't think straight. In an instant of time, my happy world had been filled with fear and I became small and withdrawn, not knowing what to do or how to cope.

Thankfully, I had the ability to put my private life "on hold" during banking hours or when someone came for healing and I noticed that by forgetting myself my happiness returned. However, these outbursts were makings things difficult for Peter. Not only was he coping with me but was feeling restricted in what he could say or do. I vowed to myself that I would never come between him and healing but there was one incident when, after healing, I let my feelings run away with me (literally!) Peter had been deep in conversation with a patient when suddenly I felt insecure. I was furious with myself but couldn't understand what had triggered it off. Therefore, in my agony, as soon as the lady had gone, I grabbed my coat and ran.

On the top of a nearby hill, I found myself sitting on a seat and crying. I knew that Peter loved me, so why was I reacting this way? It occurred to me that there was nowhere else to run! I had always seen running away as a solution, but it wasn't. I then thought, "Why am I going through this?"

Desperately, I tried to make sense of it by recalling the times when it had happened and remembered feeling this way when Peter had said nice things to his patients. Invariably, it was the start of a level of intimacy which excluded me, resulting in my feeling wretched — whereas, however attractive the patient, if I was included I was fine.

It didn't dawn on me that I was being reminded of childhood memories, when Dad had said nice things to Mum, which was a warning sign to me that they were about to become intimate. On listening to their closeness, I knew I should feel happy for them but I was hurt and upset. When they were together, no one loved or needed me!

Peter and I had been having a miserable time trying to come to terms with my outbursts. When I look back in hindsight it's crystal-clear but, at the time, he thought I didn't trust him or perhaps was accusing him of flirting. I knew it wasn't that, but how could I convince him! However, having given it some thought, I decided to go home. Thankfully, on my return, Peter offered me healing and later White Cloud gave some explanations:

☐ So many people speak to God only when they are distressed and forget Him when they are happy. When you are full of love and joy, remember to thank God for the light that has been allowed to shine on you. This will bring your "inner being" closer to the source. Never allow that moment of joy to escape you, for it is coming from the universal creative power.

As you travel along your river of life, there will always be ripples and obstacles in the way. You may think that it is not necessary to have obstacles but they are placed there for your upliftment. Also, it is essential for you to absorb the small ripples, so that you can reach a greater understanding. It would not do if all of your life you were to ride a high-horse. It would be of little use your Heavenly Father taking you further unless your soul had become more uplifted, having gained in understanding and compassion through "having been there".

Do not allow the setbacks that you receive to take you from your pathway, for it is your understanding that will enable you to help others when they come to you in need. For, when they come, you will raise them by talking from a heart that is pure but unless you have been through the experience and raised yourself, how can your Heavenly Father see that you are ready to be thrust amongst the many who need your help.

Take these experiences that cause you so much unhappiness, evaluate them for what they are worth and then you will see that they are, in fact, nothingness. After this, take the pain into your Heavenly Father's light and bless the situation that has been placed before you as an opportunity to overcome the self, and then let go and give yourself back to life. This has been an opportunity for you to walk away from the negativity that so besets you and, in so doing, God will raise you. Walk forward with courage, filling yourself with beautiful thoughts and love and allow the situation to bring you closer to God. If all people were to find the "joy of giving", what a beautiful world it would be! □

I became peaceful after White Cloud's message because, at least now, I could understand that my pain had a purpose, which was to help others from "having been there" myself and, in addition, if I could view it as a stepping stone towards God, I would be grateful for the experience rather than resenting it.

I rounded off my day by going for a relaxing walk, where I could commune with nature and thanked God for the experience, having recognised how important it had been. If I was to help others it was essential that I understood what they were going through because suffering is lonely, leaving one feeling cut off. If my words could help, then it would have all been worth while.

Shortly after this, someone gave me an interesting Christian book, which seemed to arrive at the perfect time. I have often marvelled at the coincidence that books do, in fact, turn up when we need information. It's as though, when we are trying to help ourselves, the whole universe supports us by supplying our every need. The author suggested that when we are overwhelmed with feelings of isolation, we talk to Jesus as though he was there.

Although I could recognise that these bouts of insecurity came when I was feeling excluded from Peter's conversations and knew, deep down, that I shouldn't join in because what he was saying was so important, it still didn't stop me from hurting. Therefore, when Peter became engrossed with a patient, I would escape to the kitchen by offering to make a cup of tea. Then, although I felt shy, I talked to Jesus. This was the beginning of many long conversations with him and, although they were one-sided, I felt as though he was really listening. After I had poured my heart out to him, by the time I returned to Peter I was feeling wonderful because I too had been having an intimate conversation!

As my involvement with Jesus had proved to be successful, I decided to take matters one step further. The author of the book suggested going back in time to memories that were still causing pain and to, somehow, use Jesus to create a happy ending. I had often thought how hurt I had been that Mum had saved my brother's birthday cards to her, but not mine. It hadn't occurred to me that she had saved them because Tom wasn't living at home and these gave her physical contact. I can remember, so well, feeling frantic whilst rummaging through her drawer to find the proof that she loved me. However, on re-living that scene in my mind, Jesus came out of the drawer with His arms wide open and said, "Why are you looking for pieces of paper to make you feel loved? Don't you know that I love you?" It was such a beautiful experience.

Later I thought about another incident that had caused me pain. I had run to the top of a castle to see Dad but, on arriving, had found him deep in conversation with a lady and although he had acknowledged my presence, he'd indicated with his hand that I should go away. I was so hurt that I remembered it for years. Once again, by going back in my mind, I ran back down the steps of the castle, imagined Jesus waiting for me, and ran into his arms. He greeted me with such love and affection that I totally forgot my pain. Once again, I was healed.

One of my friends went to a therapist who worked in a similar way by taking his patients back to the incident and getting them to replay it with their own happy ending. My friend found it a great comfort and shifted a lot of pain during these sessions.

Obviously, if wounds are deep and painful, I would recommend seeking the help of an qualified counsellor but if they are delicate childhood scratches which affect your relationship with others, perhaps it is time to heal them. I once heard it said that a picture paints a thousand words and I believe that by painting a fresh picture in the mind, we can wipe over the old image to create peace. Would we go on listening to an old tape that annoyed us or would we erase it, replacing it with music we liked? It's worth giving it some thought! I am not advocating going through life piece by piece. Life is for living and the best time, for all of us, is in the present but if something is keeping us stuck, perhaps now is time to move forward!

Chapter 11
THE GOOD SAMARITANS

This morning I woke up feeling happy and excited knowing I was going on a course for the bank. As well as being something different, it was an opportunity to meet new people and to see old friends, and I enjoyed learning. Also, there was something special about today — my car had been fixed. The intermittent fault had, at long last, been traced. Lightheartedly, I set off on my journey, singing at the top of my voice. However, whilst marvelling at the beauty of the wonderful morning and the blue of the sky, I wasn't concentrating on the road and was brought back to earth by a thud.

Shakily, I tried to get out of the car but the door was stuck. Therefore, I clambered across the other side to get out, quite forgetting that the faulty lock had a habit of slipping down. The frustrated look from the guy in the now "adjoining" car revealed that he was none too happy with me. I cringed at the thought of facing him but after we had talked, he was quite understanding and, having accepted my apologies, drove away. However, to my dismay, I couldn't get back into my car, so all I could do was to continue on foot.

Whilst walking, I found myself reflecting on a message that

White Cloud had given a few weeks earlier. He had asked us to see every "so-called" disaster as an opportunity for someone else to progress by allowing them to give a helping hand. I was wondering if he had known what was going to happen and was eager to see what would unfold.

On arriving at the venue, I gave my apologies for being late, explaining my predicament. Immediately, I was offered help by a gentleman who suggested we use a wire coat-hanger to juggle the lock open and, the nice thing was, whilst strolling back to the car we became friends. He was so nice that I found myself confessing that my insurance was for third-party only so he offered to come round with me to the various garages to see how much it would cost to get the car fixed. He thought that if he posed as my husband, they wouldn't rip me off and would give me a better deal. I was beginning to see what White Cloud meant. This complete stranger was taking the time to help a damsel in distress. However, the quotations were far too high for my pocket so I decided to take the car home at the end of the day and phone round later.

When we returned to the course, another gentleman offered to phone his friend who repaired cars. As a favour to him, he was sure that this friend would fix it cheaply for cash in hand. Then, to make my day, it turned out that the garage in question was only a short walk from my home. The car repairer was a super guy—kind and friendly and, although he was "rough and ready", he was prepared to help the "not so well off" people of this world by doing jobs for a ridiculously low sum. He even promised to get the car back to me the following day. He kept his word and did such a good job that I sent him many customers over the years!

That evening I received an unexpected phone call from a lady on the course to see if I'd like a lift to work the next day. I smiled to myself. Everyone seemed to be seizing the opportunity to progress. In fact, it was almost as if the accident had happened to bring out the best in them.

White Cloud greeted me warmly when he came to talk to us on absent-healing night. He was so pleased with the way I had reacted to the accident.

I must admit, the whole thing had been truly worthwhile. For the small inconvenience it had caused, it had paid dividends in friendship. Also, it was a joy to know that my "Good Samaritans" had achieved tremendous spiritual growth. It was beginning to dawn on me that being spiritual is a way of life. Peter and I rarely went to church but every day we tried to view life differently and to incorporate the teachings as often as possible.

The fascinating message from White Cloud was as follows:

☐   Every experience in life, and how you deal with it, is of great importance, for it is another lesson. An experience is a challenge for you to overcome. The whole world seems to crumble around you when something drastic happens but at times like this — stop (no matter how bad it is) and remember, "This is an experience and I am required to go through this to the best of my ability."

This is as much as your Heavenly Father would ask of you and if you do this, you will overcome. But, if you allow yourself to go into the pit and wallow in self-pity, then your Heavenly Father in His loving mercy will set it aside for you but you will have to do it all over again at some other time. It is well to remember this. I know what I am asking is not easy but life is not easy. You are here for progression.

So often, when you see someone in need, you pass by because you are not sure how you can help. But if you offer, you will progress because you overcame yourself by offering. It does not matter if your help is rejected — it was simply an opportunity for you. If you are rejected, make allowances, for perhaps you too once walked this way.

There are people who will offer you help. Give them the chance to progress. Don't turn them away and be self-sufficient, for you are giving them the opportunity to advance and, by refusing, you yourself go backwards. They have overcome by offering and you will be allowing them to go forward.

Although it is difficult, it is important for you to follow through each experience with positive thought. I know when you go through deep emotional distress, you think, "How can I be positive?"—but you can! I promise you, if you look at the situation you're in, at that moment, you can lift yourself out and rise above it and, in doing so, you will progress. But if you wallow in self-pity and apathy, then down and down you will go — praying for help. God will help and will soothe you — but the challenge will come again another day.

If only you could realise that this was a test for you because it was a necessary part of your journey. If you overcome, you will not have to go through a similar experience again. □

Chapter 12
BECOME A TWINKLING STAR IN THE NIGHT

I could never understand why some days I found it easy to be positive and happy and yet on others it seemed difficult to avoid the passing negative thoughts that arose owing to the ultrasensitive mood I was in. I used to think that my monthly cycles were getting me down but White Cloud explained it is far more than this. Although it's natural to go "up and down" with mood swings, a lot has to do with the cycle of the moon which affects not only us but the ebb and flow of the tides. Some of us are at our best before a full moon whilst others feel much better after.

Also, if there has been a war in some far distant land, a famine, or a disaster, causing people to cry out in desperation, negative waves are sent into the atmosphere making it possible for the sensitive people to be affected. On absent-healing nights, the opposite happens. Positive waves are passed out into the atmosphere as creative energy which heal and uplift those in need.

Another explanation is that when we ask to be in service to

God, sometimes it is necessary to be taken into a low ebb, where we would be in the frame of mind to experience something at a deeper level. Invariably, some soul who has been crying out will be brought to us for our help and because we have just "been there" ourselves, we can assist from a true heart. And it is our sincerity that reaches out and touches the person who is in need. In our service to God, we must ring true.

There is another reason, as I was about to find out. One day, I was particularly sensitive and tearful. I tried to brush it to one side because Peter and I were expecting one of his work colleagues to bring his wife for healing. Mary had given birth to yet another stillborn baby. This had been her third attempt to have a healthy child and, of course, she was desperately unhappy. To add to her misery, after the tragedy she had wandered the streets looking for an open church where she felt she could communicate with God, but they had all been closed. Instead of being able to deal with the pain in her own way, she had seen this as a sign that God was against her. She had completely "shut down", refusing to talk about her feelings or allowing herself to cry. Her husband became frantic for his wife to receive help.

Peter and I very often gave healing together. He would concentrate on the upper part of the body whilst I gave healing through the feet. Sitting on the floor, with Mary's feet in my lap, I tried to control the tears that were coming but I couldn't keep them away. Without rhyme or reason, the floodgates opened. Mary, on putting her arms around my shoulders to comfort me, cried too. It seems that my tears had encouraged her to give way. The men, being sensitive enough to leave us alone, allowed time for Mary's tears to penetrate her wounds and, after she had become calm, she felt as if a big weight had been lifted from her.

This experience created a special bond between Mary and myself. She continued to receive healing and when Peter gave her the "all-clear", the couple tried for another baby — this time successfully. They were so grateful that they asked Peter and me to become the baby's godparents. White Cloud explained that my prayers requesting to be in service had been heard and, in this instance, God had used me in this unusual way. Mary had needed to feel compassion for me, to enable her heart to open. Once open, God could heal her wounds, allowing the tears to wash away the impurities.

White Cloud also mentioned that when we are at the top of our wheel of life, we are in the "receiving" position for God to give to us. At times like this we are full of love and no effort is required to help others. We literally become an extension of God's love. But, although it feels good and we become bountiful and generous whilst in this heavenly state, there is little room for progression because everything is easy.

However, when we are at the bottom of the wheel, the opportunities for progression are endless. Everything appears such an uphill struggle that we have to push ourselves but, at times like this, the love earned is tremendous and cannot be taken away. It is added to the love that is already within. Sometimes, just to smile is hard work but, in that moment, it has been enough to give our soul progression. Perhaps we were so full of "self" and feeling "down" that it took an enormous effort.

White Cloud commented that whenever we overcome ourselves to help others we are like a twinkling star in the dark of the night. And we look so beautiful when we become vulnerable but still go on trying. When we strive to overcome and to do our best, in spite of adversities, our love becomes magnified, and often progression comes purely through perseverance. In one of his messages he said:

> ☐   How hard it is to help your fellowman when you are at your lowest ebb. By lowest ebb, I mean when you are physically unwell or when you are emotionally unstable because of what is happening around you in your personal life. It always seems that when you are low, things come into your life and others draw close to you, in need of help.

Become a Twinkling Star in the Night

How great is your sacrifice when you exceed yourself by giving more than you already have. At times like this, you pull from your deepest reserves to overcome the adversity that is around you. It is not easy but this is one of your greatest moments of progression. All that you give will strengthen the spirit of love that is within. Because you have given, your spirit will grow immeasurably and other souls will draw close to you for they will recognise your inner beauty and warmth, for in your lowest moments you were "as a woman with child". You were at your weakest and yet at your most beautiful as a soul.

When you are feeling weak, the tendency is to live within oneself and to have tremendous self-pity but you must draw upon your reserves to give and, I promise you, your spirit will grow a thousandfold. When you do, you will remember my words, for you will feel a warm glow inside and you will not have to pass the barriers to recognise that you have progressed — for you will "know". At this time, God's love will fill every fibre of your being.

Eventually, you will reach fullness and you will become, above all things, a tower of strength — when all of the world and earthly things will become normal to you again, and you will stride through life with your head held high. But, as I have explained, when you are at your highest, there is little chance of progression, except through prayer. ☐

Sometimes we say to ourselves, "That was a waste of time! I was so good to him and now he never comes to see me." Nothing is ever wasted. Each good thought, each good deed, each act of loving kindness, is added to your soul, making it more beautiful. Eventually that beauty shines out to the world and cannot be hidden. No matter what your age, someone will always say, "Isn't that person beautiful!" or, "Isn't that person kind or thoughtful or loving," and they will feel safe and secure in your love, wanting to know what makes you shine and why you are happy.

We went on to talk about this all week, which was good, as it prompted White Cloud to give an additional teaching which rounded it up nicely:

☐ When you find yourself in a condition of darkness, when nothing seems right, I would ask you to think, "What is happening to me? Why am I low?" and, without blaming the astral influences, to question, "Is this the 'self' factor? Am I so much thinking of self and wallowing in self-pity that I cannot overcome this?" Make an effort to bring yourself out of this apathy by bringing God's love into you. I hear you say, "How can I possibly bring God's love into me when I am so unhappy and miserable?"

I know it is difficult because when you are low nothing seems to lift you. But I say to you, you can bring in the love. You can bring in the light. Think of other souls who are sick or without food or without shelter and send forth your love to them. My promise to you is that the love of God will lift you out of your darkness, will raise you out of your apathy, and you will become as one with the universal creative love of the Father, whose love is constant and forever and always with you. ☐

Chapter 13
DON'T TAKE IT PERSONALLY

I was once asked, "Do you know why people light candles in churches?" I must admit I had no idea but was enlightened when, a couple of days later, White Cloud brought up the subject explaining that candles represent the light within each person — the light of understanding and knowledge earned through service. He said, "Allow the light that you receive in your awakening to be given to others. Become a lighthouse — a beacon for all to see." My favourite sentence was, "In the darkest corners, the brightest candles glow."

A few weeks later, a work colleague called Simon asked about healing. I wasn't aware that he was a principal member of his church and was challenging my beliefs and was unprepared for the inquisition that followed. To my amazement, instead of seizing the opportunity to talk about healing, I fled from the barrage of questions. I couldn't understand why I was so anxious to get away because normally, I'd be delighted for the interest shown but something about his manner made me feel uncomfortable and I became tongue-tied. However, I felt I had failed my duty in sharing my knowledge.

The following day, I noticed that Simon's attitude towards me had become cold and critical. His unkind remarks were out of character and, not understanding the change, I took it personally. However, on looking into his eyes, I could see that all was not well. He was moody and distracted. In the old days, he'd be cheerful and we'd be teasing each other for laughs. The office, which prided itself on a relaxed atmosphere, had been plunged into tension and despondency. Feeling worried, I asked White Cloud what I could do to restore the peace.

☐   Let's walk together so that we may put a clear perspective on all that is before us. One of the most beautiful aspects of love is kindness. The opposite of kindness is need, for where there is need you can give kindness, the nucleus of love. Give love through acts of kindness.

When you are verbally attacked by someone who does not have your understanding, they are merely fearful of the unknown and theirs is a call of need. Give forth your light in such brilliance that it will be sufficient for them to be awakened to the spiritual dawning. If you see someone who is suffering, are they not in need? Do they not cry out for the kindness of love to lift them from their emotional pain? You too have travelled the ways of this person and have recognised their need — the need which gives you the opportunity to overcome yourself by giving in kindness.

The barrier between kindness and need is "recognition". Recognise the pain of the person who comes your way, for they need the love and kindness that you produce with your light when you overcome the "self" factor. If they reject you, do not feel hurt. Although you may feel great sadness at their rejection, the love that you offer will infiltrate their need. They cannot see things as you do for they are now where you once were. They are deep within, thinking only of their problems.

Even you, with all your knowledge, still have need of others, requiring their kindness and love. For it is always a circle, one of moving forward or perhaps sometimes standing still. It is as important to give as it is to receive, for both enable your circle to roll forward to the greater understanding of God's love. ☐

This was extremely helpful because I could see that I had been blaming Simon for his attitude rather than recognising that he had a need. Therefore, bearing this in mind, I went into the office determined to get to the bottom of the problem but, feeling unable to approach him, I made discreet enquiries at management level. If I had caused offence, I needed to know. Apparently, Simon's little boy was desperately ill and could possibly die, so I was asked not to take his attitude personally. My heart went out to Simon. What must he be going through? I started to recall conversations and, from what I could gather, his church was against healing. Perhaps he had wanted to ask for help but couldn't.

Our approach towards each other softened. I never knew if the manager had told Simon of my concern but things between us improved and when his child's illness became common knowledge I could be outwardly supportive. I would show how much I cared by slipping boxes of Smarties into his coat pocket and remember so well the grin on his face when he found them. It was the grin that said everything. In a strange way, although nothing was ever spoken, it gave us a special bond. Forgiveness, acceptance—who knows!

One evening before leaving the office, the manager called me into his room. He confided that it was make or break for Simon's son and it wasn't known if he would make it through the night. I was touched by his kindness in asking me for healing prayers, and looked for Simon before going home. Without a second thought, I heard myself saying, "If you need me, just phone — any time day or night, it doesn't matter." He smiled lovingly, brushing a tear from his eye. Again, no words were spoken. The look that passed between us said it all. Needless to say, the absent-healing group worked hard that night and I awoke several times to send out my thoughts of love and healing. Thankfully, the little boy recovered.

Several months later, Simon was transferred to another branch but before he went, I was delighted when he said to his successor, "Let me introduce you to one very special lady." It wasn't so much what he said but the way he said it — full of love! It taught me a good lesson.

I learned that we need to go beyond what we see and, therefore, when dealing with customers, I tried to remember that if someone was unpleasant, to make allowances or, if they were behaving unreasonably, that I hadn't been the cause. However, I was soon tested again.

One morning, a frustrated customer took her anger out on me and, in that moment, I decided to take the verbal blows — knowing I wasn't to blame. I distanced myself, becoming the silent witness and by refusing to react, I felt uplifted. However, after she'd gone, something prompted me to go outside. My attention was drawn to a car parked awkwardly which was creating havoc. In the heat of the midday sun, a severely disabled passenger was being helped back into the car by a loving pair of hands and, as you can guess, these hands belonged to my customer. It appeared that to add to her worries, she'd had to contend with patiently waiting in the queue and by the time we had spoken, was fit to burst!

Sometimes we are tested again — just to make sure we've understood. You may be sure that if we send out the thought, "I think I handled that pretty well," we'll be inviting the challenge to be presented again but once we have learned, there's no point in going through it any more. When we've seen the situation for its true value—just a lesson on the pathway of life—and walked on to face another day, we'll be taken to the next phase and will be ready for the next classroom in this wonderful school of earth!

Chapter 14

THE BRICK!

Like everyone else, I used to make the most of the bank's photocopier as it was one of the perks of working in an office and was surprised, therefore, to be called into the manager's room to justify my actions. Apparently, a young security clerk had complained, which resulted in a total ban for private use unless we obtained permission. I was devastated because photocopy shops were few and far between and friends loved to receive White Cloud's messages. Also, I felt it my duty to share the teachings.

But the thing that upset me the most was the attitude of the security clerk. I couldn't come to terms with his arrogant manner and instead of being friendly towards him, I was hostile. Day after day I allowed him to get to my inside, becoming quietly angry and resentful.

White Cloud, having been inspired by the painting of the village pond that hung on the wall, came to the rescue by giving a wonderful teaching.

☐ In the village pond you will see the stillness of the water and because there is no agitation you will view this

The Brick!

as being peaceful. But where there is such peace, there can be little progression for in this peace is stagnation. You cannot find purification by standing still — you have to keep moving. You have to get away from the stagnant pond into the river of life—where the waters run swiftly.

Also, you cannot stay on the sides of the river setting yourself boundaries, putting yourself in bondage. Bondage creates limitation — but you have a choice. If you become static like the pond, stagnation will exist and your problems, the sediment, will sink to the bottom of your inner well. This is not healthy for you. The bad needs to be dispelled and the good needs to be shared because, for you to progress, you must overcome yourself. You must overcome the bondage that lies within.

In life, when things happen to you, causing turmoil and upset, they are stirring up the gunge from the bottom of your well but it needs to be stirred up sufficiently for the well to overflow. It must overflow for the well to become clean. When you are exposed to certain emotions which agitate you, creating strife and unhappiness, remember the agitation is a stirring-up and a blessing in its own way.

Even sickness is there to agitate this well. Whatever aggravates you is there for you to recognise, "This is what I require. Perhaps this is how I have been. May God forgive me. May God bring light and love to bear on my darkness and bless the situation that brought this about." Then, as this happens, the water in your well will expand and out will flow the darkness—never to return. And, as this darkness flows out, you will become lighter and brighter and will have gained the ability to overcome the bondage of limitation. ☐

I had swallowed a lot of anger and resentment as a child. It wasn't the done thing to show emotions and I would have been chastised if I had answered back. In my attempt to prove that I was a good girl and worthy of love, I had pushed many unhealthy feelings beneath the surface rather than acknowledge them. I knew that my inner well needed stirring up. I was fearful of speaking up for myself, of causing a fuss, and had created so many boundaries and limitations in my life. I was scared of everything —people, situations and being honest!

My version of the inner well is that throughout childhood, unexpressed emotions and hurt are pushed to the bottom. Occasionally, when a brick is thrown into the well, these emotions are stirred up which bring them to the surface. The brick can be in the form of hurtful words or events that create emotional disturbances, such as insecurity, anger, jealousy, resentment, feelings of being left out or abandonment—to name but a few! Whatever happens externally triggers off that which is within. These events or words act as a stick or brick to make the pain come to the surface.

The security clerk had become my brick and I was sure that if I could see him as a helpful tool to clean my container, it would be my first step to freedom. Also, recognising that I had been presented with an opportunity to clean my well would aid the healing process. I could see that I should thank the young man because his presence was constructive rather than destructive and, after all, if there was no muck to surface, the brick would have no effect. If the well was clean, it would only release sparkling water!

White Cloud explained that by accepting responsibility for a reaction, rather than pointing the finger of blame, we would see it as an opportunity to reach our goal of freedom. However, if we respond with anger, we add to what is already there and remain stuck.

The brick was merely the trigger, not the cause. Somewhere along the line, long before the brick was thrown, we swallowed negative emotions, becoming insecure, but by changing our approach we can see the brick as something to be welcomed rather than avoided. I was fascinated because this explanation was so simple. Not easy to do, but easy to understand.

As an effort to avoid facing old wounds, I can well understand the natural response to run away or to try to control the situation, or to manipulate the people involved. The bricks are uncomfortable and "growing" isn't easy. We may become fearful that we'll lose control or not look good or that we'll lose in some other way. Maybe we are fearful of losing the one we love or our money or our good reputation but, in truth, the only thing we lose is our freedom if we don't come to terms with the negative emotions that create restriction. So, if fear is preventing us from moving forward, what can we do? The answer is to find love. Love will always overcome fear.

I actually "do" something that I love to move away from fear. Sometimes I play beautiful music to become absorbed in it. Or I go for a walk. I may stroke the dog lovingly and, in talking to her, soothe away my fears. I also love writing and forget everything at times like this.

Some people love to play tennis, others ride bikes. Many love to paint. There's creativity with wood, clay, needlework, knitting and gardening. People love sport, horses, water activities, shopping, cooking, playing musical instruments or they meditate — I could go on forever. So many things have the ability to stir up the "love" element within, restoring balance and peace of mind and, by tapping into this source, the balm is created to wipe away fear.

This particular incident had been instrumental in changing my whole way of thinking and, at the end of the day, I was extremely grateful to the security clerk for taking me on to this greater level of understanding.

Chapter 15

THE FINAL FAREWELL

Peter and I were extremely privileged to know a delightful 27-year-old lady called Carol and although she came for healing only once, due to difficulties with transport and babysitters, her selflessness and humility made her unforgettable. When faced with a life-threatening illness, her only concern was for her husband and three small children — "What would happen to them?"

A year later we received a touching letter from Carol which implored us to visit her in hospital. I went by myself as Peter was on night duty but as I walked into the ward, I couldn't believe my eyes. There before me was her tiny form — scarcely more than skeleton. She looked at me and smiled, with a smile that lit up the room. "Fairy, you've come," she said. I tried to compose myself because I could hardly recognise her. Gently, she placed her hand in mine and asked for healing and by the time I came away, my heart was overflowing with love for this brave young lady who had so little time left to live.

The following day was Christmas Eve. Peter came with me to see her and, as we walked into the ward, her husband was waiting to present us with a beautiful bouquet of flowers, with a gift card written by Carol. Apparently it was her idea. Knowing how weak she was, we could well appreciate the effort it must have taken her to write the card, and treasured it for years. After she had asked her husband to go home to spend some time with the children, we talked to her alone. She confided that she'd been persuading him to go to the staff Christmas party, hoping he'd meet someone else. She wanted him to have a wife and the children to have a mother after she had gone. Peter and I were holding back our tears.

She requested healing for the last time, as she felt it would give her the peace and courage to face her journey. As she took our hands, she whispered, "Don't worry about me. White Cloud and Sister Anna will be waiting and I'll give them your love — in person." Peter and I came away, brokenhearted. Wherever Carol travelled to that night, she took with her a suitcase full of love and, to this day, I can't talk about her without crying. The beauty of her soul shone out, and she was selfless and kind to the last.

It was about this time that I had to face another bereavement — the ending of a friendship. My friend and I had been inseparable for years, and when she drew away I was heartbroken. The worst thing was that there was no explanation. Although Peter and I were the best of friends, this particular friend had added another dimension to my life and we were really close. I kept questioning myself as to what I had done wrong and, because I couldn't make sense of it, couldn't let it go. Knowing my dilemma, White Cloud gave a beautiful teaching to help.

> ☐ We know that when you give your friendship, you give with a true heart, with honesty, sincerity and warmth. But when you give your love, it's the giving that counts. There is always something to gain in giving but if you lose close friends, your time with them is at an end. There are many more beautiful people waiting to be brought into your safe care and keeping. This one has

found a new pathway. It is time for her to travel a new section of the river so do not be unhappy. Respect it, for it is part of your personal progression that you love — even if you feel that this beautiful friend does not love you. It is not true, for love and friendship can never be lost. It is merely a transitional period of moving on. Love must be shared.

Life would become uninteresting and, perhaps, boring if you stayed with the same group of people continuously. It is important to explore all avenues of love and friendship in order to understand and to learn forgiveness. Doesn't our Heavenly Father forgive us? Do we not accept that God's love is unconditional, no matter what, and that He will always be our friend, for are we not trying to emulate God? Look upon this as a spiritual experience. Perhaps it is a lesson for you to forgive those who you have loved and, until you have been through it, how can you understand?

The more people you meet and try to help in your everyday life, the greater depth of your experience. The more you give, the more you will receive. The more you mix, the more you will understand. Words and books are not enough. Spirituality and progression can come only from experience. Broaden your horizons. Open your mind and your heart to the love of God that you may share it — for you cannot contain it. Each time you share, you multiply that love, for a love shared grows. When you find a wonderful spiritual secret, don't keep it to yourself or it will die, as surely as the most beautiful flower.

My friendship is true because I love you unconditionally. Will you also love your friends unconditionally, allowing them their freewill, as your Father allows you yours? Do not restrict them. ☐

I know, from experience, that when one door closes, another

The Final Farewell

opens. I had spent many happy hours being content to give to one friend. Perhaps it was time to share my love and knowledge with others and let go, seeing it as a valuable lesson. It also dawned on me that, in my pain, I had judged my friend as being unkind but, maybe, she didn't know what to do or say at a time when she needed to move on. I had been so caught up in my own distress that forgiveness had not crossed my mind. Yes, I had made allowances and had conjured up good reasons to make sense of it but I was also aware that each person knows when they need to go in another direction and it's not easy to explain.

Whilst on the subject of friendships, I would like to mention that if my friends or I are weighed down by worry, we write a letter to God and place it in the Bible. It's a very satisfying way of dealing with problems that arise. However, we must ask for God's help — this is important. God gave us our freewill and, as such, cannot intervene. I always smile to myself as I write, "Dear God, It's me again." I'm sure God is delighted with this personal touch. It's best not to ask for the problem to be taken away or we won't learn from it but we need to know what to do and how to come to terms with it — and it's vital not to miss a lesson!

I find that writing a letter to God and placing it in the Bible is a wonderful way to solve a problem that keeps me awake at night but then I have to find the courage to let go in order to allow God the time to sort it out. It's human nature to hand it over and then take it back again but, having handed it over, we must trust that God will deal with it. White Cloud gave his comments on this:

> ☐ Write to God as your friend, for He is your friend and will receive your letter. When you write, He already knows your thoughts and concerns but will be honoured and privileged that you have thought sufficiently, in your heart, to write. It becomes like a prayer, and all prayers of goodness are received — especially for others. If your

question to God is one for your progression and is selfless in what you ask, God will answer it, without a shadow of doubt. For the power of God is beyond all comprehension and every letter placed in the Bible is read. □

Chapter 16
THE STORM

Upon awakening, I looked out of the window and was surprised to see that the greenhouse had moved. There had been a hurricane but I hadn't heard a thing. Then, on walking to work, I couldn't believe my eyes. Trees were lying across the road, roofs were stripped of tiles, walls were down, greenhouses were blown over and cars were smashed, and the neighbours were running around, in all directions, devastated. At the bank, we tried to open as usual, with gas lamps! It was a bewildering morning but thankfully the phones were still connected.

Little did I know that another storm had been brewing in my son's mind and it had just come to a head. To my surprise, Ivan phoned me at work, from Bristol. "Mum, I need to see you. I've got a problem." He was only 18 and although he had already left home, I knew him so well—he'd not bother me unless it was important. At such a young age, he had already learned to stand on his own feet. Therefore, right there and then, I decided to drop everything and go to him. There was no one on holiday from the office so I could easily take time off.

Without envisaging what was ahead, I jumped into the car and set off across country, believing it to be the quickest route.

My heart pounded as I ploughed my way through flooded roads, high winds and heavy rain, encountering fallen trees and road diversions. However, many hours later, I pulled over and cried. I was lost and, with the rain lashing down on my windscreen, I was frightened. I started to pray. To add to my problems, it was getting dark. My prayers helped and, having regained my courage, I continued my journey whilst singing half-remembered Sunday school hymns. I felt a bit foolish but singing had the effect of renewing my determination and, having called on God, I didn't feel so alone. Ivan will never know how much I "grew" that night. I had wanted to curl up and die but, instead, had mustered up everything that was within me. I was the hero on a great mission!

I had never been to Ivan's flat before and drove round Bristol quite oblivious as to where I was going. By now, I was almost brain-dead from the horrendous journey and was driving on autopilot, being guided as if the car had a homing device. Bristol is a big place but, by following my instincts, when I stopped to ascertain my bearings, I was outside his flat!

Not realising the extent of my exhaustion, after a big hug, Ivan took me to meet his girlfriend, Katie, who lived in a houseboat. In the pitch dark and pouring rain, I found myself jumping from a creepy deserted quay onto the wet roof of the boat that was moored to the side. The thought crossed my mind, "Even if I make it, I'll probably slide off!" I didn't fancy landing in the murky water but, having come this far, I wasn't going to chicken out.

Sitting in Katie's boat was an experience of a lifetime and I wouldn't have missed it for the world. They were smoking hash and, in the light of the gas lamps that hung on the wall, I was steadily getting higher and higher and more and more relaxed as I breathed in the smoke. The smell of the gas, the dripping rain and the sound of laughter amongst good friends was a joy in itself. I was glad I had come—grateful to be part of Ivan's world.

The next day, I sat patiently waiting for Ivan to tell me his problem. He seemed to be talking about everything and anything, except the reason he had asked me to come. Several hours later, he finally blurted out, "Mum, I think I'm gay." I must admit, I wasn't expecting this. I thought he had been going to say that Katie was pregnant or something about their relationship. "Katie knows how I feel, Mum, and, although she's my girlfriend, I think I'm more attracted to men."

Although I was unprepared for this, I tried to act normally. Grateful that he had confided in me, I put the fears that flooded into my mind on one side. I loved both my sons enough to be supportive and to accept whatever they were going through, whether it be a phase or a lifetime commitment. I knew that their experiences were necessary for their understanding of life and, as such, I should not interfere. But I came away worried. Being unfamiliar with drugs, although I had enjoyed the evening, I wasn't happy that they were being used. And, I didn't know enough about being gay to know if Ivan would be safe or whether there was a risk of Aids. My fears were for his safety.

However, a mysterious thing happened. Within weeks I was introduced to a young lady called Kathryn and, for some unknown reason, I was drawn to her. We could talk for hours and enjoyed each other's company and, in fact, became kindred spirits. Kathryn had a great influence on my life. She was trendy and lived life to the full and, although married, had a vibrant and attractive personality that drew men to her. She was good for me. I hadn't realised just how old-fashioned my appearance had become. My mother and I had continued to shop together, helping each other choose outfits but, with Kathryn's gentle persuasion, I stepped out of one mould into another. I was beginning to look and feel trendy.

One day Kathryn came to me worried. She confided that she "thought" her husband was gay, but couldn't admit it to himself. As I was still discovering about the gay culture, she found it easy to talk to me about her fears. The timing was perfect. Although I had totally accepted Ivan's pathway to be his own and had no intention of trying to change him, I was still in the process of coming to terms with it myself. So, together, Kathryn and I vowed we would put our ghosts to rest by visiting Ivan and join him in his world.

With a little help from Kathryn, I looked the part as we started going to men's gay clubs. Apparently, I was the only "mum" in sight. Dressed in Ivan's hat, sports jacket and jeans, I looked just like any other person on the gay scene. I can honestly say it was one of the happiest times in my life. We made many lovely friends — all gay, and were upset to learn that a lot of families had rejected their sons. The stories told were horrendous. The victimisation the kids had been through would probably stay with them for the rest of their lives. I was grateful for the opportunity to offer my friendship and support.

One evening, Kathryn and I heard a particularly beautiful and enlightening song that was written for the clubs. It gave a message about love and, as strange as it seems, we both picked up on the lyrics at the same time. The penny had dropped, giving us tremendous peace. It was all about the love of one person for another. It was that simple! I told myself that if Ivan died of Aids following his own pathway, knowing who he was, then that was good enough for me. I didn't want him to pretend or lead a false life and I was proud he had taken the decision to tell me, enabling me to become a part of his life. It drew us closer together.

I knew that Ivan needed to go through certain things for the experiences that were necessary for his personal growth and, by supporting him, I gained all the way. By allowing Ivan to be himself, I too was discovering new depths within me. I was much stronger than I had ever thought, was able to mix well in unusual circumstances, and had learned to bear up under stress.

Having come to terms with his sexuality, Ivan outgrew the need for hash and, with his wonderful personality and good looks, it wasn't long before he became a successful businessman, being head-hunted by insurance companies. However, whilst at work, he couldn't help but notice the filing cabinets that bulged

The Storm

at the seams with refusals for requests for mortgages, life insurance and pensions. These applications had been turned down due to the element of "high risk". Ivan quickly realised that, on average, the "high risk" applied to people like himself—gay. And having made this discovery, he decided to set up his own business.

To Ivan, it was far more than building up a successful company. His caring nature surfaced. He wanted gay people to have equal rights. He felt that they were unfairly discriminated against. If someone had Aids, to own a property would give them a reason to live. He said that couples would have something to stay together for when an argument occurred instead of giving up and leaving after the first row. He was sure that it would create the pride associated with owning one's own home. It would give gay people a future, with plans and hopes. So many wanted to settle down to the routine of a family, and Ivan was providing a service for their "nesting" instincts. They would have somewhere to feel safe and secure, perhaps for the first time in their lives. In their homes, they could be themselves without fear of rejection or eviction.

I was touched by my son's thoughtfulness. He knew, from experience, what it was like to be gay and I admired him tremendously as he revealed to the world his beliefs by acknowledging who he was. He made no attempt to hide it. Working hard to build up his business with a policy to care for his clients, he became extremely successful, winning an award for "man of the year".

I am pleased that I took the time to help Ivan through his storm. Through becoming involved, my awareness and compassion increased. Also, I felt it a privilege to enter into a world which might otherwise have remained closed to me. Later, White Cloud gave a beautiful teaching on the subject.

☐ May we talk tonight about human relationships? Will you walk with me beside the still waters of a beautiful lake and, on the lake, I see two white swans. If

89

you look towards these beautiful, most graceful swans, do they not give you peace and tranquillity? Can you tell if they are male or female? Perhaps there are those who know about the bird kingdom and would be able to distinguish but, for the majority, they would not be able to tell which was male and which was female and may I ask, does it matter? Aren't they both beautiful, giving out love and peace to the world? If you can love two birds such as these, accepting them totally without knowing their gender, can you not accept all relationships? Can you not see the simplicity of what I am saying?

Accept all people for the love they give. Each one is a child of God and, in their own way, is seeking and searching for love. When you love God's children, love them all. Just because some are different, it doesn't make them less beautiful. Maybe they have good reason to go through this experience. Everyone is here to learn lessons of progression and, I can assure you, nothing happens by chance. See now the beautiful swans — but we still don't know what they are, do we? □

Chapter 17
SEPARATION

I was missing Ivan terribly but his absence seemed to highlight the precious time spent with David — my younger son. I was determined to make the most of him while he still lived at home and put great effort into making our togetherness special. I'd sit with him for hours while he was learning to drive — getting furious when he went the wrong way around a roundabout but we'd end up giggling like a couple of teenagers. Then, when he brought home friends, we'd be excitable and noisy while playing Monopoly. He was more than a son — he was a playmate. Therefore, when he announced he was going to Australia, I was devastated. Mothers know that one day the birds will fly the nest but when they do—it's so painful!

I was grateful to Peter for his encouragement while Kathryn and I tried to make sense of our worlds, spending weekends away in Bristol. The extra time with Ivan had been a bonus. I loved his company and enjoyed talking to his friends, who were extremely sensitive and kind. It's nice to be able to stand back and watch your kids reveal another side to their personality. Ivan was dynamic in business with an immense drive to work for a cause but, beneath his facade, was modest and reserved. And, in his dealings with the gay community, he was the counsellor and friend, quietly ministering to their needs.

David, on the other hand, never found his niche in the working world and, therefore, was laid back and relaxed. But when something aroused his spiritual beliefs, he'd become passionate, wanting to share his latest discovery. His ambition was to travel the world, to study religion and to make sense of life. I always saw him as coming from another planet because he couldn't sum up the enthusiasm for any of the normal things in life, like settling down, getting a good job or buying a home! But he had the gift of patience, taking the time to listen and help whenever possible. Also, if someone was hard up, he'd give them his last penny. Later, he said, it was his destiny to wander the world and to be there for people in their hour of need and when, many years later, I met some of his fellow travellers I heard some most unusual tales of how he had come to their rescue. Both boys were totally different and yet cared—in their own way.

Through observing my sons, I noticed how much I admired their courage. They mirrored what I wanted to manifest within myself—courage—and, although I dreaded David going, I knew he was looking for an inner strength and respected his commitment to growth. However, I was going to miss him—we were so close and could talk for hours. The home was lively and happy with him around, with youngsters popping in and the phone ringing. There was always something going on. I knew that when he went it would be like losing a part of myself.

Funnily enough, it had been my secret dread that one of the boys would live abroad. Therefore, David's decision to go to Australia had thrown me into a whirlwind of fears: Would I ever see him again? Would he be OK? Who would help him when he got into difficulties? Just plain old motherly concern! I always suffered when driving away from Ivan—as though I was leaving a piece of my heart behind—so how would I feel when waving David off, not knowing if I would see him again? I always thought, "Will this time be the last?"

Separation

All too soon the day came. Taking him to the railway station (which was David's preference) was undoubtedly the biggest wrench of my life. I thought I had gone through all the pain I could handle the day I waved Ivan off when he left for Bristol, but today it was as though pain was piled on top of pain. As he walked through the barrier, still very much a young man having only just turned 18, I thought my heart would break. The fear that I would never see him again was so intense that I can well appreciate how people must have felt whilst waving their loved ones off to war. Someone once said to me that the pain of separation is the hardest thing to bear — I'm inclined to agree. It doesn't matter whether it comes from bereavement, or loss of love, or through a loved one going away to a foreign country — each pain is equal to another when love is involved and, at the time, we think we'll never get over it. My pain was no exception and, on returning home, the place seemed awfully empty without David. And as much as Peter tried to console me, I felt empty too.

Turning out their cupboards was a heartbreaking experience in itself. Little hats came out of the wardrobes, crumpled pieces of paper with childish writing now seemed like precious treasures, and the empty beds and lonely guitar only served to stir up memories. On kissing each item tenderly, how I wished I'd made time for that extra goodnight kiss. So often they had asked me for one more cuddle before going to sleep and I'd made my excuses to hurry away — and why had the nine-o'clock news seemed more important than that additional hug? The feelings were indescribable: a mixture of gratitude, loss, love, gentleness, pride and regret — all intertwined. We can't turn back the clock but how I wish I had made more of our time together. We never think it's going to end but, when it does, memories are all we have left. The boys had brought colour into my life and it was going to seem pretty drab without them.

On looking back, I suppose that separation is a form of bereavement but isn't recognised as such. Perhaps my pain had been intensified because David left home to go abroad and I hadn't got used to being apart from him. But, at the time, I was remembering my friends whose son had died and was beginning to realise the extent of their suffering. Although my loss was no comparison, it had put me in touch with their pain and I could understand a little more.

My compassion had increased in other areas too. I was concerned for the parents of the young lady who went missing whilst working for a firm of estate agents. We put the entire family in the healing book and, in fact, became genuinely upset for any lost child. Loss of any kind became more meaningful. And, in addition to responding with sympathy, I would find myself emotionally involved and, having taken it to heart, would pray for them with a deeper understanding. White Cloud gave this explanation:

> ☐ You are constantly taken back to points of suffering and being reminded of pain and heartache. You are learning compassion and the only way is through experience. What sort of life would you have if you sailed through without suffering, without love, without emotional pain? Surely, these are the stepping stones towards greater understanding. You are here to become love. You are here to become light. Each one of you can become a candle to many — so that your light may reach out and touch those in need.
>
> Life can be beautiful even in your pain and sorrow. Just remember that by going through every experience, those who need your help will not be talking to empty ears. They will know you care and by sharing your understanding, you will allow their candle to burn bright — which will add to the illumination of the whole.
>
> It is only through finding compassion for everyone that you can make your own candle grow bright. Your soul, this beautiful part of God that lives within, has

Separation

chosen to go through many experiences. Your greatest progression towards love is when you give to others through identifying with them, no matter what their problem — however small. Their problems are like mountains to them but your words can transform their mountains to a lush meadow, full of beautiful flowers. They need your love, time and understanding. Who can they turn to? Who can they identify with? They need the sincerity of your words. ☐

With these teachings, I decided to put on a brave face and to stop thinking about myself. I was happy and excited for David and his adventures, and I could save up for a visit. It wasn't the end of the world and, although I couldn't foresee it at the time, eventually David was to open another chapter in my life when I joined him — many years later. His leaving turned out to be a beginning for me, and not an end! Also, upon reflection, I came to appreciate how lucky I had been to have shared so many years with my sons and knew, from White Cloud's reassurances, that I could never lose their love. However, his advice on the subject helped me put the matter to rest:

☐ If you have pain, give thanks, for when it comes you are given the chance to rise above it and to have a greater understanding. Bless the pain that you receive. I am referring to emotional pain — to the loss of a loved one. I would ask you to mentally place the situation into God's light, asking for His help along your river of life. You know it is a necessary part of progression. You can either go beneath the water, or rise above it. But, by blessing the pain, the help and guidance will come in mysterious ways.

If you are asking for help for others, remember, "Thy will be done." If it is God's will, they will overcome the adversities but it may not be part of the plan.

However, the mere fact that you have asked and given your love and healing thoughts will make their pathway easier. It will help them to accept their difficulties and to continue their journey with courage. But remember, make a mental picture of the situation when placing the condition into the light. ☐

I found this to be extremely helpful and made time to go for a walk, where I could use the sunlight to assist me with bringing the situation into God's light. After appreciating what I had learned, and having given thanks for the enlightenment, I felt a flood of love enter my heart and my peace return. I had dealt with the problem and was free to move on.

Whilst reflecting on this subject some time later, my mind drifted to another observation which I would like to share. I had often wondered why I had mourned the death of my dog even more than the death of my dad. After all, I loved Dad in every possible way. But I had already missed and longed for Dad's company when the initial separation took place, when I left to get married. Initially I had pined for him, taking every opportunity to go back to the family home and it had taken many years to make the final break — whereas with my dog I'd had to contend with her death and separation at the same time. She was very much a part of my life and, when she died, there was a gap.

It dawned on me that there were two issues here and not one. Separation and death. With my dad, the separation had already taken place, the wound healed and the gap filled. What do you think?

Chapter 18

THE FOUR SEASONS

One of the problems with losing the boys — and that's how I saw it — was that I didn't have a worthwhile role to play anymore. I'd been a gentle but firm mother and whilst allowing the boys their individuality and freedom, there had also been a fair amount of discipline and my word was final. It was an area of myself where I felt totally fulfilled as a human being. And, although flexible, behind the scenes I was very much in control. This part of my life had given me a way of expressing myself as a person who shone in her own right. When it was over, it was as though I'd lost my role in the scene of a play.

I had always left the counselling side of healing to Peter. He and I were very much alike in so far as he too was gentle but firm and his patients loved him dearly for it and, although I helped, I didn't like to interfere. Even though I knew I had the gift of healing, I didn't want to tread on Peter's toes. It was "his patch" and he loved his patients. I felt that if I overstepped the mark, I would be depriving him in some way. It was a difficult situation, knowing I wanted to be useful and give healing too.

I started attending courses on alternative therapies, hoping that I could contribute in other ways. These were in connection with crystal healing and the use of Bach Flower Remedies. I so wanted to be of assistance that, after my studies, I eagerly offered my services. Encouragingly, Peter made every effort to slide over to give me an equal role in our world of healing but, to my disappointment, the bank changed my hours and I was no longer free in the afternoons to accompany him. I felt tremendously sad when I realised that the healing scene was about to close as well. We had always done healing together but now Peter was about to go solo.

With my commitment to healing but being unable to participate, I felt trapped. An innocent remark from Peter such as, "The healing went well today" would set alarm bells off within me and, instead of being happy, I'd be thinking, "I'm not needed any more." Overnight, our togetherness went and I was envying Peter his success and the freedom to follow the path of his choice. I was the outsider, fitted in whenever possible. I knew he was doing his best to include me, and therefore I felt petty and small! He was a good man and didn't deserve this.

Another problem had entered. Peter was not a well man himself and had become increasingly ill whilst coping with shift duties. As he had been deprived of a good night's sleep for so many years, I had volunteered to carry on working to enable him to take early retirement. Financially, therefore, I was tied to a job that paid our bills. It hadn't worried me living on less as we had everything we needed but, unfortunately, the monthly pension was not enough for me to leave the bank.

Peter became increasingly happy in his life, chatting to the neighbours, walking the dog and giving healing, but I was no longer part of this. With my hours having changed we became separate and, by the time I came home, the things we had shared were over. I felt desperately unhappy as we settled down night after night to watch the television. Was this all my life was about? The bank had started to concentrate on marketing, so now I couldn't even promote healing! Peter, on the other hand, had just been through another enjoyable and meaningful day. Sadly, I came to the conclusion that my involvement in the healing scene was now obsolete.

It was a bewildering time. I knew I should be happy that Peter was fulfilling his ambition but, instead, I was empty and desolate. His happiness served only to highlight my misery. We had always done everything together but now I was excluded and felt wounded and hurt. And, although I should have been grateful for the fact that Peter took over the household chores, suddenly I had no role to play in that area either. When I returned home to our immaculate house there was nothing to do. It was as though my life had no direction or purpose. Peter's, however, was full to overflowing.

I even resented not being able to join in the walks that were so meaningful to me. I didn't feel we were married any more. We had shared everything, the chores, the walks, the upbringing of the boys, the healing, the friendships that healing brought but now — patients were coming and going and names were being mentioned of people I had never met, and I didn't belong in Peter's world any more. Our relationship had dissolved right before my eyes and there was nothing I could do about it. Peter was not only going solo in healing but in every other department.

The other thing that was nagging at the back of my mind was that although I had been really happy at work, I knew that it was time to move on. Every time I approached the bank, instead of being filled with joy, I saw it as a prison from where there was no escape. It was as though someone had switched off my light and, as hard as I tried, my heart wasn't in it anymore. I didn't enjoy marketing and, with the pressure to produce results, I was no longer given the time to be myself. It had become a workplace rather than a platform where I could share my spiritual life. The magic had gone. Ironically enough, when I did eventually leave the bank many years later, it was due to redundancy. I left because I had no role to play there either but it was too soon for me to know this and, for the time being, I could see no end to the situation.

I knew then that it was time to get out of my relationship with Peter. I loved and respected him but this overwhelming feeling to be free to pursue my own destiny was so great that I had begun to begrudge going home or going to work. The big act of appearing to be a loving housewife or an efficient cashier was exhausting and I began to feel terribly old. Everything was an effort. My arms and legs ached and became like lead weights. On the few occasions I joined Peter for healing, I didn't want to be there. I felt dead! I was merely a fly on the wall, observing as opposed to taking part. I didn't belong and, furthermore, I had become the intruder.

To the rest of the world things were fine but the confusion was all too much for me and I couldn't confide in Peter. Before this, our life had been an open book but with his ill health, traumas would bring on chest pains and although, having left work, he was more relaxed, it was going to take him a long time to get over the years of stress-related work and it hadn't crossed our minds that he was close to a heart attack.

I felt so disturbed that I cried out, "Dear God, please help. Peter's a wonderful guy but I need to be free." Peter gave me as much freedom as possible but it wasn't enough. I wanted to be me and not an extension of someone else. I was fed up with taking the back seat. I wanted to be the person behind the driving wheel. I needed to steer my own car and to make my own decisions and to come and go without restrictions. Was this so selfish?

For me, being married had meant putting my partner first and I had often left something in order to return home, as arranged. But now I wanted to be independent and to be out there, doing my own thing. I wanted to be a healer in my own right and to share the teachings in my own way and not to be answerable to Peter for my whereabouts. He had complete freedom — so why shouldn't I? I became the naughty child,

The Four Seasons

rebellious and, Peter's word, "stroppy", in my endeavour to break away from a loving parent. For the first time in my life, I was breaking free from the mould of trying to please!

Peter couldn't understand the change in my personality. Until now, we had been such a loving couple and I had centred my life around him. Before, I had seen his protectiveness as care but now, I saw it as a mild form of control. He made allowances and tried to adapt, forgiving my irrational outbursts, but he was puzzled at my behaviour. It's all so clear now but it certainly wasn't then. It was a confusing mess!

As far as I was concerned, I had outgrown the need for a protective father but as far as Peter was concerned, I was still his "Fairy", whom he adored, and who was simply going through a bad patch! I might add that today we can laugh about this but, at the time, it was unbearable. We had been so "one" and so "together" that it was devastating, not only for us but for all those who knew and loved us. On reflection, I was taking a giant step towards my personal growth but it wasn't viewed as such then. There and then, we couldn't see the wood for the trees!

It was as though I was in the winter of my life but, optimistically, I knew that spring was just around the corner. However, quite unable to express myself, I was saddened when my familiar stammer returned. On noticing my struggle, Mum said, "Why don't you ask Peter for some healing?" I explained that I couldn't because the confusion was about Peter. Also, I was full of shame and guilt. Compassionately, she offered to pay for me to see someone else — which I gladly accepted. Little did I know that my life was about to change, yet again!

On relaying the story to the therapist, he smiled reassuringly and told me not to worry. From what he could gather, many chapters in my life had closed and it was natural for me to feel old but, as soon as new ones opened, I would feel life surging through me again and my youthful and vibrant personality would reappear. What a relief!

I suppose it's like the seasons. I had felt I was in the winter

101

of my life but, instinctively, I knew that spring was just around the corner. Perhaps the summer was when Peter and I were in full bloom, when we had togetherness, and the autumn was when life began to change, indicating that it was time to move on. Nothing remains the same and, although we fear change, sometimes it's for the best. For life is about growth and, as such, we need to go on growing throughout the four seasons in order to reach our full potential.

Undoubtedly, there was a time when Peter and I were in the summer of our lives. We really were the happiest couple I knew but now, although the parting wasn't obvious, it had taken place. We had been as one but now were two. The therapist explained that it was natural for my speech problem to resurface as my roots of security had been threatened. It was understandable when seen in this context.

I had been fortunate in my choice of therapists because mine could interpret dreams. And, although I insisted that I couldn't remember dreams, he assured me that I could. Hoping that he was right, I decided to give it a go, so before going to sleep at night I sent up a request to recall my dream. To my amazement, every morning, I recounted a similar one. Quite simply, I was going abroad, travelling towards a red sky! After excitedly relaying each dream to the therapist, he said, "I think you should go abroad. What place springs to mind in connection with a red sky?" Without any hesitation, I replied, "India."

Chapter 19
WHEN IT'S RIGHT, IT FEELS RIGHT!

"Operation India" went into action and, to my surprise, Peter was totally supportive. He knew how delicate the situation was between us and I think it was a gesture towards saving our marriage. He really was a beautiful man, and still is, I might add, but wasn't so superhuman that he could drop his protectiveness: he insisted that I went with an organised group—which was fine by me. I was just grateful for his support.

It wasn't going to happen overnight as we needed to save a lot of money, but I was eager to make plans. It didn't occur to me to go to a travel agent as I had never been abroad but I decided to seek the advice of a friend who had just returned from India. This friend was full of her trip—explaining that she had been to see a well known avatar called Sathya Sai Baba. As I had never heard of him, she sent me a magazine.

By chance, another friend told me about Father Bede Griffiths, an elderly priest who had taken up residence in India to form an Eastern–Western religion. I found this fascinating because, prior to this, I hadn't heard about any holy men in India.

It was as though the word India had miraculously conjured up names out of thin air. Therefore, on seeing the pilgrimage information advertised in the Sai Baba magazine, I decided to apply, pointing out to the organiser that although I was not a devotee, I was interested in joining a group if there was the slightest chance that I could visit Father Bede.

Within a couple of days I received an answer saying that there was a group going to India in eleven months and that another lady within the group also wanted to visit Father Bede. To my amazement, the lady in question, Judy, lived only a few miles away. Peter and I both saw this as a sign that this particular trip was for me and, even more so, because we had been led to it so easily. Additionally, on meeting Judy, we were in for another surprise. It was as though we were having a reunion as opposed to meeting someone new — we felt so comfortable with each other. It did, however, leave us wondering what the purpose was behind our trip.

My therapist was like a breath of spring. The sessions were so beneficial that I felt I was closing the door on the winter of my life. New doors were opening and, as predicted, I was feeling alive again. The friendships that unfolded were like buds on a tree — beginning to bloom with the approach of summer. The phone was ringing and, to my delight, the calls were for me. At first, it was a bit frightening. I had only known myself as Peter's wife, the boys' mother, my mother's daughter or a bank clerk — but never just me!

I was fearful of being myself, wondering if people would like me. It seemed natural at school to have friends but this was different — there were expectations and I didn't know if I could live up to them. Also, although I had begun to move out of the role of trying to please, I had a long way to go. I still needed to please in order to feel loved and, in fact, with new acquaintances, I was so eager for the friendship to be a success that, at times, I'd allow myself to be a doormat. Then I'd end up feeling used — but it was all new to me and I was willing to learn. I was on a voyage

When it's Right, it Feels Right!

of discovery which, in the main, was to discover myself. I knew my weaknesses but not my strengths.

One of the most difficult lessons for me was learning to say no. Sometimes a friend would phone to ask me a favour and, although I received immense pleasure from helping, it was not always convenient or, maybe, I was too tired—but didn't have the courage to refuse or explain. I was so grateful for their friendship that I'd go to any lengths to keep it. It didn't dawn on me that I could be liked even when I said no! Also, I didn't have the confidence to disagree so I rarely made a fuss about anything, but there were times when I was quietly hurting. Outwardly, I'd put on a good show but I knew that there was something wrong because I didn't feel good inside. However, now I know, when it's right—it feels right!

I hadn't realised the importance of loving myself or being true to myself. These were entirely new concepts that I hadn't yet acknowledged. If they had been mentioned, I hadn't taken them on board because I was not ready. I thought that being spiritual simply meant giving to others.

Also, I hadn't fully understood the complete meaning of the word intuition — the promptings from within that would have wanted me to look after myself, as well as others. I wasn't prepared to listen because my need for love was so great that I would ignore this inner guidance, judging it as selfish. I didn't understand that this voice of loving concern was part of God and, as such, would have my welfare at heart as well as the welfare of everyone else. Also, it didn't cross my mind that I could be kind to myself because I had always relied on receiving kindness from others.

Although Peter was doing his best to give me every possible freedom, having encountered immense suffering in foster homes, he was more secure and at his happiest with a daily routine. The opposite had happened with me: I had been stifled. My mother and father had held so tightly to the reins of their little girl—lest any harm should come to her—that I was craving to break away from any form of control. Also, when I was helping people, I didn't want to clock-watch or to have to justify my actions. Therefore, an inner conflict was emerging as to whether to please Peter and help within a framework or whether to be true to myself by following my instincts.

But, apart from this, other things were presenting themselves to me. One of my greatest challenges was when I was asked to do the introductions on stage for a seminar concerning alternative therapies. Although I agreed, I was so frightened that my speech would block that, before the big day, I spent nearly all night on my knees praying for help as I was determined to overcome my fears and take up the challenge.

On arrival at the seminar, my nerves were so bad that I couldn't speak but, thankfully, one of the organisers asked me to announce that coffee was being served and, although by now I was almost paralysed with fear, some minute part of me found the courage to "just do it". Then, a miraculous thing happened. A greater force took over and I found myself talking naturally, as if my body didn't belong to me any more. At the end of the day, I came off stage full of gratitude and thanks but, almost immediately, my speech froze again as if to prove the immensity of this power.

After this, there was no holding me. I was asked to attend many meetings to give talks and although I was always worried about my speech, when it came to the crunch, the words came out clear and true. I was learning to trust in this infinite power, which was there for the asking. And may I remind you it's there for you too—you only have to ask!

Chapter 20
AN INSPIRATION TO MANY

It was a tremendous blow to us when Peter suffered a severe heart attack. Hospitals, doctors' surgeries, operation waiting lists, pills, anxiety and stress were all part of our new experience! It was unbelievable! I now knew why White Cloud had repeatedly said we have to go through something in order to appreciate the full extent of the suffering. I could write an entire book on this subject. Now we were at the receiving end of what our patients had endured. They had tried to explain but, for all our listening and with all our understanding, we weren't prepared for the long drawn-out two years that followed. White Cloud had given many messages about experiences but one in particular stands out in my mind.

☐   You are here upon a journey of life which you personally undertake. You will not learn about life simply by watching television. You would be like someone in a glass bottle, travelling along the river of life seeing and observing everything but joining in nothing. You would feel safe and secure where nothing could touch you. But beware: the glass could shatter and you would be thrown into life once more. It's better to travel in the river itself, exposed to all things, knowing that God's love will keep you safe and sound. Your spirituality will keep you buoyant!

You must have experiences — even the ones you want to reject. Negative and positive, action and reaction, are part of life and symbolic of advancement. You can hide, avoiding all contents of life, seeing those around you living their lives—going through anguish and uncertainty, exhilaration and ecstasy, but you cannot participate or understand if you have encapsulated yourself in a glass bottle. Nothing will touch you. Nothing will affect you. You will have merely become the watcher! What a waste of time. You might just as well have stayed where you were.

How can you understand illness, unless you have been ill? How can you understand pain and suffering, unless you have suffered? How can you understand the complexities until you have been there? We would all like to slide along in the glass bottle at times, protected, watching the world slide by, unaffected, not wishing to experience these things for ourselves, but what would you learn? These experiences give understanding which, in turn, gives compassion — for, as you know, compassion is another aspect of love.

Do not allow yourself to wallow in self-pity. Try to go through this experience to the best of your ability. You hollow out for yourself, with pain and sorrow, a well which will one day be filled with joy and happiness. The deeper the well, the more it will hold, but it cannot hold much unless you experience all aspects of life. Remember, there is no substitute for experience. □

Whilst Peter was waiting for open heart surgery his health deteriorated rapidly and I took over many of his patients for

An Inspiration to Many

healing. This proved to be a tremendous growing time, requiring sensitivity on my part not to overstep the mark which could cause Peter to feel redundant. Having been used to shining in his own right, it must have been a challenge for him to take the back seat and now he was experiencing for himself how difficult it was to be "the watcher", without interfering. However, I found it beneficial insofar as I was becoming stronger and a healer in my own right. I enjoyed passing on the teachings and gained more knowledge, simply by sharing.

It was during this period that we were introduced to a delightful baby called Natalie. She suffered with a spinal condition which took away the use of her arms and legs. Also, she could not support the weight of her head. Her enchanting smile and honest eyes revealed the purity of the world she had left behind and, as she was still very much part of the spiritual kingdom, it was like being with an angel.

Devastated by their daughter's condition, the parents were willing to try anything to prevent Natalie from dying and we were their last hope. Although Peter was unable to channel White Cloud during this period, he was inspired to talk to them. He explained that some babies merely touch earth for the benefit of mankind and that parents had a choice. They could either wallow in self-pity or take up the challenge and go forward so that the child's life would not be wasted.

Natalie had a condition that was rare in this country and for which there was no cure. They had been presented with an opportunity where they could either pioneer and raise funds to find the cause of the illness, becoming shining lights to many, or they could bathe forever in their tears. If they chose the latter it would be understandable, but if they chose to become pioneers, it would take great courage.

Initially Natalie's parents had decided to adopt a child from a Third World country, but after her death they campaigned to such an extent that, to this day, an annual fund-raising march is still held, involving many who have been placed in similar circumstances. They formed a support group where advice and tears could be shared but, because their lives were so busy with counselling, they pushed aside their own need to adopt a baby. Instead, they became content to be in touch daily with the many babies who would benefit from their help. Their bravery and commitment meant that Natalie's life was not in vain.

Another very special person came into our lives at this time who also was an inspiration. Mike was an amazing and outstanding character who made the most of life. I saw him as a big man, with a big heart but, in his words, he was a rogue and a lady's man! A fall off his horse brought on MS, a most debilitating illness. Mike was at the mercy of his wheelchair, crutches and a reliable pair of hands. Through healing, Peter and I came to know and love not only Mike, but many other beautiful people who helped. It was an opportunity for everyone to grow!

Mike's illness brought him on to the spiritual pathway and with great enthusiasm he ploughed his way through *The Course in Miracles*. Also, he wouldn't dream of missing an opportunity to listen to White Cloud — however awkward the journey. Witnessing the struggle he encountered getting in and out of his car and climbing the steps into our bungalow, without losing his sense of humour, was a wonder in itself. He said that every day he thanked God for the illness that had brought him onto the spiritual pathway and in touch with such beautiful people.

His life became full to overflowing. He joined practical philosophy classes, which were a source of inspiration to him, and read as many books as possible in connection with spiritual awareness. It was a magical time for all of us because everyone put themselves out to attend the discussion evenings, where Mike became the life and soul of the party and, through Mike, we experienced the brotherhood of man. We had complete unity and purpose, where we all pulled together to make Mike's short life on earth more pleasurable.

Just being with Mike and sharing his enthusiasm for life was an inspiration in itself. His light became so bright that it lit up the room. He gave out more love during this time than most give in their entire life and, by not complaining, he inspired others to remain strong. It put everything into perspective.

When he died, the church was packed with friends who genuinely loved him as the rogue with a golden heart. Funnily enough, he was a silversmith by trade. He may not have been perfect but, if love is the key, Mike fashioned for himself the most perfect key to enter the kingdom of heaven.

Chapter 21
EVERYTHING PRESENTED IN THE RIGHT ORDER

The year slipped by very quickly and before long, I was setting off to India. I had decided to cancel the trip but Peter wouldn't hear of it. However, friends and neighbours offered to keep a watchful eye on him so I departed with a peaceful mind. I was extremely grateful as I longed for the space and time to reflect.

The one thing that persistently overshadowed my life was my desire to be free, and I needed to look at this whilst in India. Perhaps the distance would enable me to see things clearly. I hadn't been able to discuss it with anyone because, at a time when Peter was ill, it seemed selfish. However, I had a plan of escape in my dreams! I would imagine Peter falling in love with a caring nurse who had the gift of healing in her hands and who would centre her life around him. She would adore him, be happy to assist with healing and would love and respect White Cloud's teachings as much as myself!

On arriving in India, I felt completely out of my depth but my saving grace was a lady called Sheila, who suffered with M.E. She was a member of our group and, as I could give healing, it

Everything Presented in the Right Order

was suggested we share a room. We clicked immediately and, to my delight, she lived near Peter and myself. Over the weeks, we confided in each other, enabling me to put things into perspective. I thought of her as a gift because she contained so much wisdom and I respected her opinions. In fact, we became like sisters who were comfortable with each other and, being a nurse, she gave me an insight into Peter's illness, which helped tremendously. We were perfectly suited for one another. She enjoyed the healing and my version of White Cloud's teachings, and I enjoyed her company. Little did I know that Sheila was the nurse I had conjured up in my dreams!

I was to discover that an ashram is where a community of people spend time in contemplation, meditation and prayer. There are workshops on yoga and meditation, should anyone care to join, or talks and lectures should anyone wish to attend. They weren't compulsory and I didn't feel the need to get involved. However, my chosen pastime was getting up early in the morning so that I could give myself over to absent-healing. Also, I loved listening to the dawn chorus and watching the sunrise as the sky turned to a crimson red as I became one with God and the mystical atmosphere.

Whilst visiting the ashram of Sai Baba, I overheard a lecturer talk about an educational programme called "Education in Human Values". For some unknown reason, I was prompted to pause for a while and listen. Apparently, Sai Baba had said that he would like to encourage the values of love, peace, truth, right conduct and non-violence to be taught in schools from an early age, as part of the school curriculum. These values could then be taken into adult life and, hopefully, contribute towards world peace. Books suitable for schools of all denominations had been compiled with hourly lesson plans without promoting religion. I liked the sound of this because religion is personal whereas human kindness often needs a little encouragement. I was so inspired that I decided to explore the possibility of getting a Teacher's Certificate on my return to England to enable me to take the programme into schools.

Things were looking up. Something had aroused my interest which could possibly offer me a future, but I still hadn't found the answer to my personal problem. Peter had shown me so much kindness that I couldn't contemplate leaving but, when he was fully recovered, would it be in order for me to become independent? I didn't want to hurt Peter or to do the wrong thing.

Then, an extraordinary thing happened. I met an old lady who seemed to be expecting me. I had just been praying in the chapel, asking for help. On coming out into the sunlight, I noticed her sitting on a wall and, without thinking, wandered over to sit by her side. Acknowledging me, she said, "You want to talk, don't you?" She appeared to be a kindly soul with infinite wisdom. Without attempting to make a decision for me, her advice was to write a letter to Sai Baba and give it to him. Trusting in his ability to see things clearly she said that if he took the letter it meant I could leave Peter but if he refused, I should stay!

Thanking her, I hurried off to get down to work. At least now I had direction. The following day, Sai Baba came on his usual rounds to shower blessings upon us. Tentatively, I handed him my letter but, after a moment's thought, he refused it! My heart pounded and all I could think was, "I have received my answer and must stay with Peter." However, a little while later, I started to doubt. "Did he really know what was in my letter?"

I decided to stay in the courtyard after the others had left, to regain my equilibrium. Also, it was such a beautiful morning that I wanted to use the sun's rays to focus my absent-healing thoughts. When all was quiet, I closed my eyes and went deep within but a change in the atmosphere caused me to open them. To my amazement, Sai Baba was standing there, patiently waiting for me to become aware of his presence. Once again, he solemnly shook his head and, glancing towards the letter that lay by my side, made a gesture indicating that I shouldn't leave Peter. After

Everything Presented in the Right Order

this, he walked away, without speaking a word. I was puzzled but grateful and, in that moment, I became resolute to abide by his guidance.

As I left the courtyard, the old lady approached me, as if she had known what had taken place. "I feel certain that Sai Baba will come and explain to you, in a dream. Sometimes he uses a dream to clarify a complicated message because it will have a lasting effect, whereas if he had spoken it might confuse you. He never enters a dream unless it is his will and will instigate it only for specific reasons. If I am correct, see me tomorrow and I will interpret the dream for you."

Now I was excited, for these unusual events meant that I was receiving the help for which I had asked. Therefore I retired to bed early that night in eager anticipation! On reflection, the lady must have been acting from intuition, which would account for her miraculous timing and accurate guidance. As predicted, the dream came, so I sought her out to receive the interpretation.

At first, Peter and I were sharing the same car (the car symbolising our life together). Then, Peter and I were in different cars, driving our own. My car turned right (which meant it was right for me) and, although Peter's turned left, it didn't mean it was wrong for him because it was my dream. It purely signified the parting of the ways. However, the road was so cluttered with other cars (other lives) that I had to drive my car awkwardly, balancing it on two wheels in order to get through. The car turned right again, onto a road with less traffic, and after another right turn the road became clear. The fact that I had taken so many right-hand turnings, coming back to where I began, indicated I would achieve wholeness.

The dream continued. At the end of the road, Sai Baba was waiting. He simply said, "You've made it at last!" He offered me a silk robe, with Sheila modelling it, which I refused. Apparently I turned down a wealthy way of life. (There are days when I would love to have that scene repeated so that I could change my mind!) Then, I was offered an enormous book which I accepted. On opening it, all I could see was the letter E. Not understanding its significance, I said, "What does this mean? Why is there an E on this page?" Sai Baba replied, "EHV. That's what I want you to teach. Education in Human Values."

The lady pointed out that my dream was a personal interview with Sai Baba. She felt it indicated that I would leave Peter one day but the time was not right yet and perhaps my lesson was patience. She assured me that if my move was for the good of mankind and for the spiritual growth of everyone concerned, a way would be found where no one would be hurt. She told me to let go, and trust!

I thought, by now, that I knew why I had been guided to India but there was more to come! I was falling back into my role of trying to please and, in the heat of the day, it was I who was queuing for water! Instead of being human, like everyone else, I would try to be superhuman to make life easier for the other group members, who resented it! It was making them feel uncomfortable. Sheila tried to warn me, saying that she too had once been like me, making herself ill, but I didn't catch on. Then, one day, they could take no more and made their feelings known. They felt I was being a martyr and wasn't being true to myself. Apparently, I was showing signs of resentment. This was true but I hadn't realised it showed!

For a while, it gave me a lot to think about and I cried bitterly, resenting having my faults highlighted. I thought, "I don't know who I am any more!" People-pleasing had been a way of life. However, on reflection, I knew I had been ignoring my inner guidance. Perhaps this was the meaning of the words, "To thine own self be true."

Thankfully, Judy had not been a party to the confrontation and suggested that we get away for a while to visit Father Bede. She was obviously inspired because we discovered that Father Bede's teachings were based on honouring the intuition! Our visit was timed to perfection. We didn't know much about this charming 84-year-old English Benedictine monk who had formed his own ashram in India but we both fell in love with him. He was delightful and told us that, should we have the need to talk, his door was permanently open to us. He blessed our healing, joined us at meal times and gave us individual attention throughout our stay.

He explained that our intuition is guidance from God and, because of this, we should listen to it. Furthermore, the intuitive part of ourselves is the feminine side and the action part is the masculine side so by listening and acting on intuition, wholeness is achieved. This made sense because I had already heard of the Yin and Yang, which has the same principle.

In one of our conversations, Judy said to Father Bede, "What do you think about healing?" With a special smile, he replied, "My dears, I try not to think!"

He explained that he used a mantra to still his mind and when we asked which one, he said he repeated the Lord's Prayer over and over again. He confessed that the only time he had been able to still his mind was when he had been unwell with a stroke! It had been a beautiful experience for him as he had been able to enter into the lotus of his heart. He approved of healing but emphasised that, as most wounds are internal, each and every person has the ability to heal themselves by going within.

He also mentioned something which I found interesting. Apparently one day a young man owned up to having a mistress as well as a wife and asked for advice. Father Bede replied simply, "Do well by both of them!" His unique and brief answers made a lasting impression on me.

He also talked about going into the woods! He explained that on reaching a certain age, having been through the earthly progression of growing up, going to work, creating a home and, perhaps, bringing up a family, there would come a time when it would be an advantage to develop spiritual awareness. This was the concept behind "going into the woods". He pointed out that if someone wanted to join us, they would need to be supportive and have a similar goal but it wasn't necessary to enter the woods alone. However, it would be no good entering with someone who wasn't prepared to devote their lives to spirituality. Perhaps this was why Father Bede's ashram was in the woods because, although we had the support of one another, we also had the time and space to contemplate.

Judy and I had time to reflect as we sat by the river, resting our backs against the eucalyptus trees. Everything about the ashram was serene and natural, unlike Sai Baba's ashram which was busy and concrete. I later viewed Sai Baba's ashram as a massive workshop whereby, through circumstances, we faced our shortcomings. By mixing with so many people, emotions were stirred that required our attention. Queuing for food, sharing accommodation and needing privacy — it all brought up frustration, resentment, anger, jealousy and envy, to name but a few! It's not an easy place to be, whereas Father Bede's ashram offered individual accommodation and consisted of a few monks, with only a handful of people, which made the whole experience blissful. We felt loved and nurtured there, with plenty of alone time to go within, but still had the benefit of wonderful teachings as and when required.

Judy and I talked it through and decided that there were many ways to get in touch with our intuition: perhaps through meditation or music, singing, writing, dance, art, walking, tuning into nature or in moments of stillness. We knew it could manifest as a strong feeling, a hunch, an image, or through an inner voice but, normally, it was experienced as a gut feeling.

My mind wandered back. Maybe when I had been guided to leave my sons to their own devices, I should have taken heed. Wanting to save them from disaster, I had interfered against my gut feelings, playing the role of rescuer. I may have been preventing their growth by taking their responsibilities upon my shoulders. I had enjoyed being the hero, gaining their love and gratitude but perhaps it was now time to earn my own love and respect by honouring my quiet voice within. It was going to be a challenge!

Everything Presented in the Right Order

But it had affected other areas of my life too. By ignoring my gut feelings, I had become a doormat! I had allowed myself to be used and abused throughout my life. I was always the willing pair of hands that worked long after everyone else had gone home. How much longer was I prepared to be a martyr and go on leading a double life, one of saying yes instead of saying no. I needed to listen to that gut feeling when it cried out in despair, rather than ignoring it. It was about time I was true to myself in every possible way.

On reviewing my stay in India, everything had been presented to me in the right order. Sheila had contributed enormously through listening and being supportive. The old lady, who had popped out of nowhere, had guided me towards finding the solution to my problem. Sai Baba had given me direction and had blessed me with a dream. EHV had aroused my interest to foresee a future in teaching. My shortcomings had been exposed to me, highlighting the fact that they needed my attention now, and Father Bede had been the icing on the cake in showing me the importance of following the intuition.

I came away feeling fulfilled and ready for the final stage of my journey with Peter. I didn't know what the future would hold. I only knew that I should trust and let go. The dream had shown me that I simply had to flow and to negotiate each and every obstacle as it presented itself. However, before I finish, I would like to mention the captivating 80-year-old monk at Father Bede's ashram who, whilst walking in front of Judy and myself, had turned around and said, "Do you know, I still find it difficult to say no!"

Chapter 22
THE PARTING OF THE WAYS

On my return to England, I read an excellent book by Beverly Hare which pointed out something that I didn't understand. Assertiveness is to do with regaining one's own power as opposed to controlling someone else. Her suggested ways of saying "no" helped me tremendously and, to my delight, the natural reward that resulted from honesty was self-esteem, with a bonus of self-respect. I would recommend anyone who has difficulty in saying no to attend an assertiveness course or to read a book on the subject. It's made such a difference to my life.

I couldn't afford to leave the bank to pursue a career in teaching but decided to find out as much as possible about the Education in Human Values programme. The lessons were designed to give self-esteem to children and to build up their confidence. The children were encouraged to see the good in everyone and everything, and to view kindness and consideration as a matter of priority. They were taught simple techniques to listen to another's problems and to talk about their own, without embarrassment. They were shown the value of forgiveness and how good it feels to make allowances and were made aware of

The Parting of the Ways

the importance of honesty. I was impressed because it was such a beautiful concept.

Although I wasn't qualified to go into schools, I came up with the idea to introduce the programme to the parents and decided to create wonderful courses suitable for families. They were to be fun, with games, songs, circle dancing, activities for the children and a guided meditation, and were to include a topic of discussion to encompass the values where everyone could join in. When I had compiled the courses, I started by inviting a few friends. The evenings were so enjoyable that two opportunities were presented where I could hold regular monthly meetings, with families participating. At long last, I had found my niche and I was contributing something of my own.

Peter, however, was going through a bad patch. His life was centred around hospitals, the side-effects of medication and, being unable to do the things he loved, he had entered into the dark realms of his mind. He was caught up in fear and dreaded the operation and, although he knew for certain that life was eternal, he was worried about passing into the spirit world. However, one of White Cloud's messages helped, which I should like to share because I feel it will benefit others who face a similar experience.

☐ Can you remember being born? Can you remember the pain, anguish and suffering of first coming to this plane of earth? I think the answer must be no. Not one of you can remember and I say this to you so that it will remove all fear. When you leave and return to your Heavenly Father, you will know no pain. You will be as you were when you were born upon this earth. Have no fear, for there is nothing except joy at the end. At the end of life is a new beginning and when the veil is drawn, you will see many loved ones. These loved ones, who have been with you on your journey of life, will be there to welcome you back. They will have been with you in your highest and lowest moments, and will have shared your joys and sorrows.

I would remind you that you can take nothing from this life, save the love that you have earned. There is no death. You merely travel from one condition to another, from life to life and, one day, as each one of you prepares to slip into the next journey, a wonderful experience will be waiting for you. It will be far more wonderful than the experience you had in coming to earth, into the dark realms, for as beautiful as your earth is, it is as nothing compared with the spiritual kingdom.

Life does not stop, my children. You do not stand still when you reach the spiritual realms, for as soon as you have acquired sufficient knowledge, then to work you must go, for you will dearly want it. But it will be a different kind of work to that which you have known upon the earth.

The spiritual kingdom is a realm of love, like each band of a rainbow. You will go to where you have earned the right, through giving of yourself. When you reach the filtration point, you will pass safely to the plane of existence that you have earned. You cannot go too high or it would be too bright for you but, through developing the spirit within, you shall walk from one glorious band of the rainbow to the next. It is as simple and as complex as this.

Your whole life on earth is based on the realisation that "I am not this body". It belongs to Mother Earth and to Mother Earth it shall return, whereas, the spirit will return to the spiritual kingdom. ☐

I thought my heart would break as Peter's big blue honest eyes conveyed to me the fear he was feeling as he was being wheeled away to the operating theatre. I ran to the hospital chapel and prayed. However, without warning, a flood of guilt surfaced, along with the rush of tears. My mind went back to

The Parting of the Ways

when I had acted like a rebellious teenager — fighting for my freedom. I hadn't been the perfect wife so how could I forgive myself if Peter died? In my rational moments, I knew I had done my best but, there and then, I could remember only how selfish I'd been.

I wanted to stay at the hospital but they advised against it, saying that it would be more helpful if I went home. So I returned to the empty bungalow and started to rummage through White Cloud's teachings to find something that would give me comfort. I needed to forgive myself but didn't know how. I knew that White Cloud had talked about forgiveness but it hadn't meant much to me because at that time I wasn't feeling guilty. Obviously he had known this was going to happen. White Cloud had been a gem! What would I have done without him? He had pulled me through so many difficult situations, which is why it has been vital to share his teachings.

I found his message on forgiveness, which helped immediately. I would like to share this because, after taking the time to work on myself, I found the peace to get me through the long night that followed.

> ☐ You have great difficulty in forgiving yourself. "How can I forgive myself for the things I have done?" But, I say to you, if you bring this deed or action or thought into your innermost being and reveal it to yourself, remembering that God's light and love is within you, what you are doing is laying this deed at the altar of love, where God's light can shine upon it. For your innermost being will accept the truth and make allowances for your humanness. God does not judge you for He loves you unconditionally and, as His love is within you, you too have the power to forgive yourself and to love yourself unconditionally.
>
> If you can forgive another, can you not forgive yourself, for are you not as equal as your brother? Take

yourself and the thing that you have done, bringing it into the innermost part of yourself that is God — into the part of you that is universal love. Show yourself what you have done and the mere fact that you have acknowledged this deed: the darkness will be absorbed by the light. What you are saying to the God within is, "I have travelled in darkness and now I seek the light. I wish to remove myself from this veil of darkness. I wish to reveal to myself that which I have unwittingly and unknowingly committed."

There is no need to go on punishing yourself. You are the only one who will stay still, or progress. If you can recognise, whilst on earth, the wrongs you have done to your fellowman and to yourself, you will indeed have travelled far.

My prayer would be, "Father, please remove this darkness so that I may become illumined — that I may advance towards your beautiful world of light. Help me to understand forgiveness and then to forgive myself. Help me to love myself so that, in turn, I may be more loving to others."

As mortals of earth, no one is perfect. Everyone is human with human frailties and, as such, we must make allowances. Once we have forgiven ourselves we can, more easily, forgive others because, having recognised our own humanness, we will then be in a position to recognise their humanness. Also, we will not be so swift to judge once we have recognised our own shortcomings. ☐

Thankfully, Peter pulled through and my guilt was forgotten along with his fears, but it was a good experience for both of us because our compassion increased a thousandfold for others who were faced with a similar ordeal. I really wouldn't wish that experience on anyone. But on reflection, as healers, we needed to be put in touch with those who we were trying to help.

The Parting of the Ways

Things returned to normal and Peter began to give healing. Although our patients were pleased, I was bewildered once more. There was still no room for me within the marriage. I had enjoyed my role as healer and caring for Peter throughout his crisis and doing the household chores and walking the dog, but now I was surplus to requirements. Peter was longing to get back to the routine that had made him happy but the only light in my life was outside the home. To me, the home was a base where I could be fed and watered but it wasn't enough. I needed a purpose within the home.

Our finances had been made easier with the addition of another small pension but it hadn't occurred to me that I could leave the bank. Therefore, without exploring any other possibilities, Peter and I returned to where we left off before the heart attack and, in spite of the fact that my gut feeling was telling me it was time to move on, I ignored it. However, because I turned my back on this inner guidance, I was plagued with a sense of hopelessness and anxiety. How could I explain to Peter that I thought it was over between us?

With the arrival of his 60th birthday, I returned home from work to find a dear friend waiting for me. It was Sheila. She had lost my telephone number but, as someone had recently given it to her, she had been able to regain contact. Peter had answered the phone when she called and, remembering the high regard I had for Sheila, invited her over to give me a surprise.

As I watched Peter and Sheila tease one another with obvious ease, I could see that they had a wonderful affinity, but I wasn't surprised, as I too had felt comfortable with Sheila. She was funny but sensitive, with a bubbly personality that matched Peter's to perfection, and looking in from the outside, they seemed an ideal couple! What was I thinking? I quickly reasoned that, as we return to earth in groups, we probably were part of the same group and Sheila was a kindred spirit.

However, within a couple of days we met another kindred spirit, but this time, it was me who felt the strongest connection.

Her name was Alex, and after being introduced to her through healing, we were as close as two dear friends who had been reunited after a long separation. We seemed to have so much to say to each other — as if we were catching up on lost time. Also, there was a sense of urgency to disclose to one another our spiritual discoveries. We later found out that, in a previous life, we had shared the same mother which meant, of course, we were sisters and, in this lifetime, we were channelling the same healing guide, called Naomi.

A few months later it was Christmas and, whilst waiting for Ivan to join us, my heart was as heavy as lead. As hard as I tried, I couldn't get into the Christmas spirit. David was abroad and I was missing him and my feeling to move on was now so strong that I couldn't get it out of my mind. I should have trusted in my intuition and spoken earlier but I was terrified of hurting Peter. Ivan was surprised when he arrived home to his normally cheerful Mum to find me putting on a brave face. He could read me like a book and needed only to look into my eyes to know that something was wrong. After I explained he said, "You must be honest with Dad, Mum, and tell him what you've told me. We'll discuss it over the dinner table, like grown-ups." His comment made me smile!

It was the most horrendous Christmas dinner I have ever sat through. Ivan broached the subject and, without interrupting, Peter listened. I thought he would respond with distress and, perhaps, with retaliation, but he simply said, "To your own self be true, Fairy." We thought it would be easy to say goodbye but, a couple of weeks later, when we finally went our separate ways, the pain was unbearable. We were like Hansel and Gretel who had been together in the woods but we had grown up and were now childhood sweethearts saying farewell.

Alex offered me a home until I could sort myself out and Peter started to see Sheila, as a friend. Perhaps this is why Sai Baba had shown Sheila to me in my dream. Peter and Sheila were so compatible that when I saw Peter's sparkling eyes, I had no sense of guilt, and Peter didn't feel guilty either as he watched me bloom and grow year after year. We knew we had done the right thing.

We remained the best of friends, without any jealousy, or quarrels over who took what from the family home, which was eventually sold. What became of Peter and Sheila and what became of me? Well, I invite you to read the next story!

But before I go on my way, I would like to leave you with the words that have been a source of inspiration to me: "To thine own self be true." I've had to learn the hard way but my life would have been far less painful if I had taken heed of these beautiful words.

All that is left for me to say now is God Bless you all.

Anthea is now writing two more books:

- *Tales from a Glastonbury Landlady*
  (the next part of her story)

- *Nothing Happens by Chance*
    (spiritual teachings from White Cloud)

Also by Anthea Mitchell

The Glastonbury Guide to Peace and Happiness

A workbook to foster self-esteem and for running courses on the subject. Based on the author's own experiences, it covers such topics as affirmations, negativity, intuition and handling fears.

It's a highly practical 48-page workbook with easy-to-apply principles for leading a more fulfilling life. *"A breath of fresh air!"*

ISBN 0-9033-5101-4   £4.95

Orders and enquiries telephone (01458) 83 3467